Apple Pro Training Series

Getting Started with Aperture

Apple
Certified

Apple Pro Training Series: Getting Started with Aperture
Copyright © 2006 by Apple Computer

Published by Peachpit Press. For information on Peachpit Press books, contact:

Peachpit Press
1249 Eighth Street
Berkeley, CA 94710
(510) 524-2178
Fax: (510) 524-2221
http://www.peachpit.com
To report errors, please send a note to errata@peachpit.com
Peachpit Press is a division of Pearson Education

Editor: Serena Herr
Production Coordinator: Amy Parker
Technical Editors: Adam Green, Dion Scoppettuolo
Technical Reviewer: Orlando Luna
Copy Editor: Karen Seriguchi
Compositor: Amy Parker
Cover Design: George Mattingly

ISBN 0-321-42275-9

9 8 7 6 5 4 3 2 1
Printed and bound in the United States of America

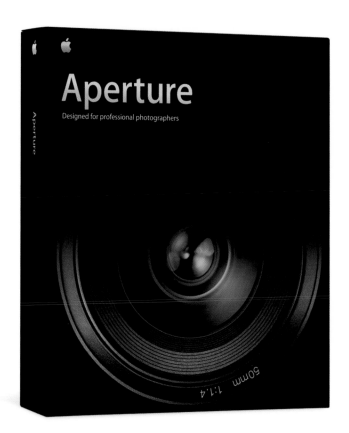

Contents at a Glance

Table of Contents

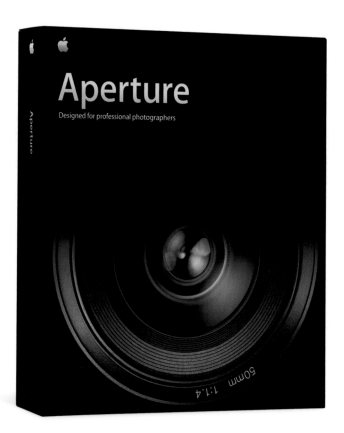

Getting Started

Welcome to Aperture, the revolutionary postproduction workflow tool for professional photographers.

The lessons in this book are based on the tutorials available in PDF format on the Apple Pro Training DVD that comes with the Aperture software. Peachpit Press has expanded those tutorials and published them here for readers and teachers who prefer to have more in-depth tutorials in printed form.

The Methodology

This book is an introduction to Aperture. It aims to get you up to speed with Aperture quickly by giving you a good overview of the application and a basic level of familiarity with its key features.

The lessons emphasize hands-on training. Each exercise is designed to help you learn the application in a real-world context, starting with the basic interface and moving on to more advanced techniques.

It will be helpful for you to start at the beginning and progress through each lesson in order, since each lesson builds on information learned in previous ones. The book assumes a basic level of familiarity with the Mac OS X operating system.

Course Structure

The book is made up of eight step-by-step, project-based lessons, the equivalent of about eight hours of training. All of the sample images used in the lessons are included with the Aperture software.

Lessons 1–4: Photo Management

The first four lessons focus on image management. Designed specifically for professional digital photographers, Aperture is an enormously powerful tool for handling some of the most time-consuming and tedious tasks of professional photography. In this section, you'll learn to sort, compare, and rate images; apply keywords and metadata easily; display images in compelling ways for clients; organize images into categories for different intended uses; and archive images in a way that's easy, secure, and intuitive.

Lessons 5–6: Image Processing

Lessons 5 and 6 start out with the basics of image editing in Aperture and move on to cover some of Aperture's more advanced image processing features, such as the Spot & Patch, Lift, and Stamp tools. You'll learn to make basic adjustments—those for exposure, levels, white balance, cropping, straightening, highlights and shadows, red-eye, and noise—as well as more complex adjustments, such specialized color effects and flawless blemish retouching and blends.

Lessons 7–8: Print and Web Publishing

Lessons 7 and 8 focus on proofing and publishing: the culmination of the Aperture workflow. You'll start by taking a comprehensive look at exporting image files from Aperture for use in other applications and for print and Web output. Then you'll create a web gallery for client review and a web journal for online image display. From there, you'll explore some of Aperture's print output options by making a contact sheet and a printed book. Finally, you'll take a brief look at color-managed workflows within Aperture.

System Requirements

Before beginning to use *Apple Pro Training Series: Getting Started with Aperture,* you should have a working knowledge of your computer and its operating system. Make sure that you know how to use the mouse and standard menus and commands and also how to open, save, and close files. If you need to review these techniques, see the printed or online documentation included with your system.

Minimum system requirements for Aperture are:

- Power Mac G5 with a 1.8 GHz or faster processor; 15- or 17-inch PowerBook G4 with a 1.25 GHz or faster processor; or 17- or 20-inch iMac G5 with a 1.8 GHz or faster PowerPC G5 processor

- Mac OS X version 10.4.3 or later

- 1 GB of RAM (2 GB recommended)

- One of the following graphics cards: NVIDIA GeForce 6600 LE, 6600, 6800 Ultra DDL, 6800 GT DDL, 7800 GT; NVIDIA Quadro FX 4500; ATI Radeon X600 Pro, X600 XT, X800 XT Mac Edition, X850 XT, 9800 XT, 9800 Pro, 9700 Pro, 9600, 9600 XT, 9600 Pro, or 9650; ATI Mobility Radeon 9700 or 9600.

- 5 GB of available disk space for application, templates, and tutorial.

About the Apple Pro Training Series

Apple Pro Training Series: Getting Started with Aperture is part of the official training series for Apple Pro applications, developed by experts in the field and certified by Apple Computer. The series is the official course curriculum used by Apple Authorized Training Centers, and offers complete training in all Apple Pro products. The lessons are designed to let you learn at your own pace. Although each lesson provides step-by-step instructions for creating specific projects, there's room for exploration and experimentation. You can progress through the book from beginning to end, or dive right into the lessons that interest you most.

For a complete list of Apple Pro Training Series books, see the course catalog at the end of this book, or visit www.peachpit.com/applebooklet.

Apple Pro Certification Program

The Apple Pro Training and Certification Program is designed to keep you at the forefront of Apple's digital media technology while giving you a competitive edge in today's ever-changing job market. Whether you're an editor, graphic designer, sound designer, special effects artist, or teacher, these training tools are meant to help you expand your skills.

You can become a certified Apple Pro by taking the certification exam at an Apple Authorized Training Center. Certification is offered in Aperture, Final Cut Pro, DVD Studio Pro, Shake, and Logic. Successful certification as an Apple Pro gives you official recognition of your knowledge of Apple's professional applications while allowing you to market yourself to employers and clients as a skilled, pro-level user of Apple products.

Apple offers training courses at Apple Authorized Training Centers worldwide. These courses, which use the Apple Pro Training Series books as their curriculum, are taught by Apple Certified Trainers and balance concepts and lectures with hands-on labs and exercises. Apple Authorized Training Centers have been carefully selected and have met Apple's highest standards in all areas, including facilities, instructors, course delivery, and infrastructure. The goal of the program is to offer Apple customers, from beginners to the most seasoned professionals, the highest-quality training experience.

To find an Authorized Training Center near you, go to www.apple.com/
software/pro/training.

Resources

Apple Pro Training Series: Getting Started with Aperture is an introduction to
Aperture. It is not intended to be a comprehensive reference manual, nor does
it replace the documentation that comes with the application. For more information about program features, refer to these resources:

- The User Manual. Accessed through the Help menu, the User Manual contains a complete description of all features, along with recommended
  techniques and procedures.

- The Apple Pro Training DVD tutorial included with the Aperture software.

- Apple's Web site: www.apple.com.

- *Apple Pro Training Series: Aperture* (ISBN: 0-321-42276-7). A comprehensive self-paced book and the official course curriculum for Apple Pro
  Training Level 1 certification classes. www.peachpit.com/applebooklet

1

Goals   Become familiar with the Aperture interface

Import images, create a project, and choose a location for your photographs

Define the difference between a digital master file and versions of that image

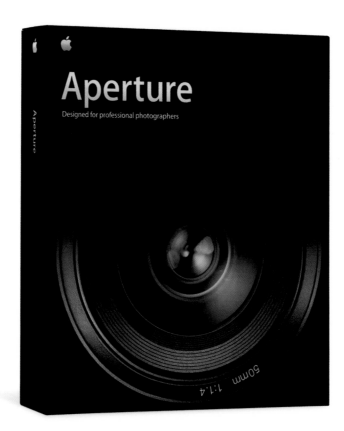

Working With the Aperture Interface

Welcome to Aperture, the revolutionary application for managing and editing digital photographs. This is the first of eight step-by-step lessons that will guide you through the process of importing images; sorting, ranking, and managing images with unparalleled efficiency; editing and retouching your selected images professionally; and exporting, publishing, and archiving your images.

Lesson 1 focuses on the Aperture interface, as well as how to import images from various sources. It also explains Aperture's ingenious master/versions file architecture, which enables you to make virtually unlimited versions of your RAW image file without significantly increasing your storage needs.

Preparing the Project

Before you start, you'll need to install the Aperture software on your hard disk. Refer to the Getting Started documentation for instructions on setting up your Aperture system and installing the software.

Once you have the Aperture application installed and your computer, display(s), and peripheral devices set up, you're ready to begin this lesson.

Opening Aperture

There are three ways to open Aperture:

▶ Double-click the Aperture application icon, located inside the Applications folder on your hard disk.

▶ Click once on the Aperture icon in your Dock.

▶ Double-click any Aperture project file.

For this exercise, you'll open Aperture by double-clicking the application icon.

1   Locate the Applications folder on your computer. Double-click the folder to open it.

The folder opens to reveal the applications installed on your computer.

2 Double-click the Aperture application icon to open Aperture.

When you first open Aperture, you're greeted by a Welcome screen listing several tasks and options that are useful when you're getting to know the application. "Start using Aperture" is selected by default.

We won't be using the other options during this tutorial, but if you'd like to come back to this screen the next time you open Aperture, leave the box checked at the bottom of the window.

3 Click Continue to start using Aperture.

A menu appears asking if you want to use Aperture when you connect your digital camera. If you decide not to use Aperture, you may have to install other software to download photos from your digital camera. This selection can be changed at any time in the Preferences panel.

4 Choose Use Aperture.

Next you'll see the Sample Project Import window, which asks if you want to load the Sample Projects. Since we will be using the images in the Sample Projects for the exercises in this tutorial, you should load the images.

5   Click OK to load all the Sample Projects. Aperture will begin importing the projects, and a progress bar will appear. When it has finished importing, click Continue.

6   When Aperture opens, you will see the main window displaying the Standard layout. In the upper left-hand pane, click the disclosure triangle next to the Sample Projects folder to reveal its contents. Click to select the Tibet project.

7   Press I to display the Inspectors panel.

Exploring the Main Window

Before we dive into the first exercise, let's take a quick look at the Aperture interface.

The main window opens in the default layout, which you will routinely use when working in Aperture. You can modify this layout at any time to accommodate your preferences. There are seven primary interface elements in the main window:

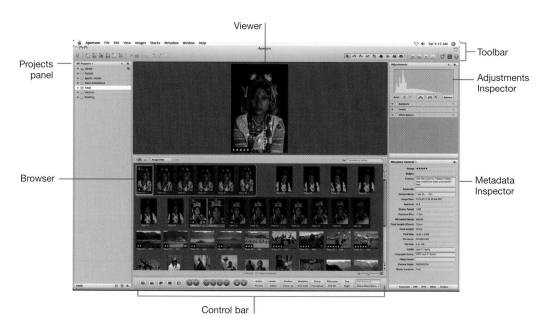

Projects panel The Projects panel is where you organize your images, using projects, albums, and Smart Albums. Smart Albums let you automatically find and group images based on search criteria that you specify.

Browser The Browser provides an efficient way to sort through large numbers of images quickly. It displays thumbnails for all the photos in a given project, folder of projects, or album. You can use the Browser to select, move, copy, and sort your images. You can even categorize your images in the Browser by applying ratings and keywords.

Viewer The Viewer is where your images are displayed. You can view and compare up to ten images at the same time. You can also utilize a second display to view images in a continuous desktop that extends across two screens, or work in full-screen mode on the second display.

Control bar The control bar gives you quick access to tools that allow you to rotate, navigate, magnify, rate, and apply keywords to your images.

Toolbar The toolbar, which runs across the entire top of the main window, provides easy access to buttons that let you create projects and folders, organize images, apply adjustments, navigate through Aperture windows, and view image information. The toolbar buttons also let you reveal Adjustments heads-up displays, or HUDs, which are floating panels of contextual controls.

Adjustments Inspector The Adjustments Inspector lets you apply image adjustments and view adjustments that have been applied to an image.

Metadata Inspector The Metadata Inspector is where all the information associated with an image is displayed. You can view filename, version number, caption text, and file size. You can also view and enter industry-standard metadata like EXIF (Exchangeable Image File), and IPTC (International Press Telecommunications Council) information.

> **NOTE ▶** In Aperture, there are multiple ways to perform most tasks. The flexibility of the interface lets you work the way that's best for you. Commands can be implemented from pop-up menus, via mouse clicks, or by keyboard shortcuts.
>
> There are also multiple levels of undo in Aperture. If one of the steps in these exercises does not yield the result you want, just select Undo from the Edit menu, or press Command-Z.

Importing Images With Aperture

The first step in any photo editing workflow is to import the images you want to work with, whether from a camera, an external drive, or another location on your computer's hard disk.

Before importing, however, you need to understand two things about how Aperture works: the difference between a master image and versions of that image, and the location of the master Library.

Master Image vs. Versions

Aperture is nondestructive. Your original image is always preserved as a digital *master file*; any adjustments to the image are made on *versions* of the original image.

It's important to understand that while versions show up as thumbnails that *behave* like image files in the Projects panel and the Browser, they are not actually new image files. Think of versions as proxy images. In reality, they are little bundles of math that instruct Aperture to apply certain adjustments to the master file. You can create as many versions of the master image as you want.

The beauty of this design is that, since version files are quite small, you can make countless versions of a full-resolution RAW image without significantly increasing your storage needs, and you can always return to your untouched master file.

If you make an adjustment to an image, there is no need to rename it or to perform a Save As operation. The version you created is saved within your project. Of course, at any time you can create a full image file that incorporates the adjustments you made to a version simply by printing or exporting the version.

Later in this lesson you will practice creating versions of a master image.

Library Location

Your master images are located in the Library. The default location of the Library is the Pictures folder of your home directory.

If you have a dedicated external drive for images, you will need to change the location of your Library. Since Aperture consolidates the images you import and stores them all in the Library, it's important to locate your Library on a disk that has an adequate storage capacity.

1   Choose Aperture > Preferences.

2 Change the Library Location path in the text field at the top of the Preferences window. Click Set and navigate to the new Library location on your external drive. Click Select.

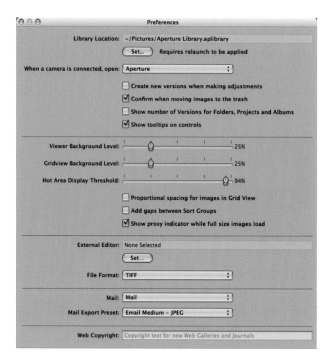

Importing From a Camera or Card Reader

For the exercises in this tutorial, we'll use images that are provided with the Aperture Sample Projects library. However, you may want to include some images of your own to work with, so let's take a moment to import some of your own images into Aperture.

NOTE ► Aperture supports color-managed workflows, managing ICC color profile information for your input and output devices. If you are using a color-managed workflow, it's important to calibrate and profile your devices before importing your images. For more on color-managed workflows, see Lesson 3, "Professional Web and Print Output," or the Aperture documentation.

You can import images from three places: a camera or memory card, an existing iPhoto Library, and an existing folder in your Finder. We'll start by importing from a camera.

1   Connect your camera's memory card reader or connect your camera to your computer.

Notice that your Projects panel has changed to include the Import pane, and a visual guide in the form of an arrow indicates the import path and destination. This arrow is called the *Import arrow*. You can import your images into a new project or an existing project simply by clicking to select the chosen project in the Projects panel.

2   Press Command-N to create a new project, and name your project *Lesson 01 Import*. The Import arrow will shift to indicate that Lesson 01 Import is the new import destination.

NOTE ▶ If you don't select an existing project, Aperture will create an untitled project for you.

Grouping by Timestamp While Importing Images

One nice feature of Aperture is that it gives you the option to group your images according to their timestamp information, that is, to *auto-stack* your images, while you import. This is extremely useful, as you can automatically group photographs that were taken in the same timeframe. Often, photographs taken within a minute of each other are of the same subject, and it can be helpful to group them together.

We'll explore stacks in more detail later in this tutorial. For now, let's just take a quick look at how to auto-stack images during import.

3   Below the main Browser area is the Auto-Stack slider. The slider determines the maximum interval in seconds between images in a stack. Click the slider marker and move it to 15 seconds.

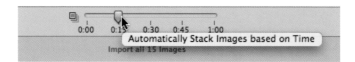

The images you import will now be automatically grouped according to their timestamp. Any images taken within 15 seconds of each other will be grouped together into a stack.

4   Click the icon to the left of the Auto-Stack slider to Close All Stacks.

Adding Metadata While Importing Images

Another useful feature in Aperture is the ability to add metadata as you import your images. Let's take a moment to look at the Metadata Inspector, and add some metadata to the images you are importing.

5   Click any image currently displaying in the Browser to select it. (Here, we show sample images, but your images may of course be different.)

Notice that to the right of the main Browser, the Metadata Inspector has expanded to include sections for image, time zone adjustment, and name format information, as well as other metadata. You can use the Inspector to enter, view, and edit your images' metadata during import.

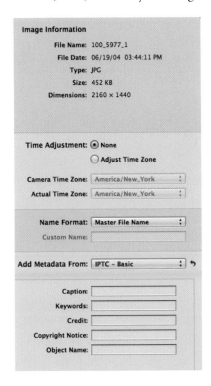

At the top of the window, the Image Information section lists basic information about your image. Below that is the Time Adjustment section, where you can alter the time zone of your images' timestamp.

The next section, Name Format, lets you enter a more descriptive image name. You can choose from various naming presets or edit them to create your own.

The bottom section lets you add detailed metadata information such as copyright notice, credit line, keywords, and object name. You can choose to view different preset metadata categories by selecting the Add Metadata From pop-up-menu. You can choose from a number of templates, and you can enter as much or as little information as you choose.

Note that several of the presets allow you to view and edit an image's EXIF and IPTC data. The EXIF information includes a wide range of camera settings such as shutter speed, date and time, focal length, exposure, metering pattern, and flash information. The IPTC information, which can be embedded in a digital image by most image-editing applications, includes information like captions or copyright notices.

> **NOTE ►** Aperture also lets you easily apply a customized watermark to any image or group of images. See the user's guide for details.

Of course, metadata information can also be added and edited after you import your images, and we'll discuss metadata in more detail later in this tutorial. But it is often handy to enter at least basic information about the shoot while you are importing the images.

For now, let's practice entering metadata during an import.

6   Click anywhere on the gray background of the browser, press Command-Shift-A to deselect the image you highlighted in the previous step. Then type your name into the Credit text field of the Metadata Inspector.

7   Click the Import All button in the lower-right corner to begin your import.

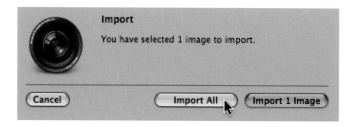

NOTE ▶ You can choose to import a single image, a selection of images, or the entire contents of your card or camera. If you choose to import the entire contents, make sure you do not have any images selected prior to your import—Aperture will assume by default that you wish to import them all.

The progress indicator to the left of your project illustrates the progress of the import.

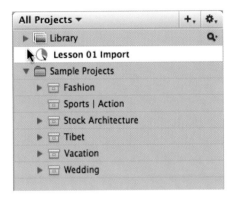

As the images are imported, they are displayed in the Browser. Notice that any images taken within 15 seconds of each other are grouped into stacks, and all images carry your name in the credit line of the Metadata Inspector. Note that you can adjust the Auto-Stack grouping parameters at any time simply by selecting the images and adjusting the Auto-Stack slider.

Aperture imports a master file into your Library and simultaneously creates a version file and a thumbnail of each image. You can begin to edit your images as they appear.

Aperture is a QuickTime-compatible application, so it supports standard QuickTime-compatible formats in addition to file formats such as RAW, JPEG, JPEG2000, GIF, TIFF, and PNG (for a comprehensive list please refer to the user's guide).

TIP ▶ Digital master files, especially RAW images, tend to be extremely large. Since your projects may consist of hundreds or even thousands of master files, it's a good idea to invest in a high-capacity external hard drive for optimal performance.

8   Click either Erase and Eject Card, or Eject Card.

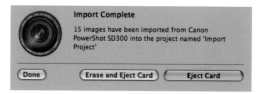

> **Import Complete**
>
> 15 images have been imported from Canon PowerShot SD300 into the project named 'Import Project'
>
> (Done)   (Erase and Eject Card)   (Eject Card)

NOTE ▶ Aperture stores your images, so it's safe to erase the contents of your card once the import is complete. If you wish to leave your card or camera mounted, then simply click Done.

Importing Images From iPhoto

If you have an existing iPhoto Library, you can simply and easily import your images from that Library into Aperture. Aperture gives you the choice of either importing all your images into a single project called iPhoto Library, or using the Import window to customize the import. Aperture maintains your iPhoto organizational structure along with your iPhoto albums, keywords, ratings, and adjustments.

1   Choose File > Import > iPhoto Library.

2   Navigate to your iPhoto Library Folder in your Pictures folder and click Choose.

3   Click Use Import Window from the Import iPhoto Library as Project dialog.

TIP Aperture duplicates your iPhoto Library when you import your images, so you can save disk space by deleting your iPhoto Library after you import it, if you no longer wish to use iPhoto for managing and editing your images.

4   Navigate to your iPhoto Library to set it as the source of the import.

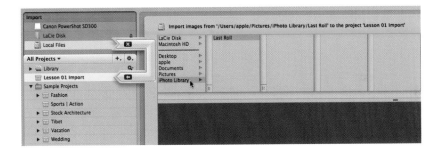

5   Click Import Images.

You can also import specific iPhoto albums or film rolls.

1   Choose File > Import > Images.

2   Navigate to the appropriate location in the iPhoto Library folder and click Choose. Note that Aperture will import any RAW files managed in iPhoto, rather than proxy .jpg files.

Importing Images From the Finder

If you already have images in your Finder, you can import them directly into Aperture, automatically creating Aperture albums that match your existing folder structure. You can either create a new project or import them into an existing project.

1   Click to choose an existing project or choose File > New Project.

2   Choose File > Import > Folders Into a Project

3   Navigate to your image folders and click Open.

You can also import individual files.

1   Choose File > Import > Images.

2   Navigate to your images in the column view display above the Browser.

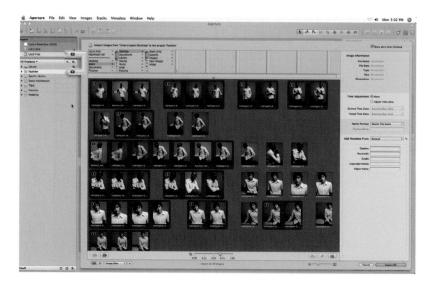

Notice that the import interface for individual files looks similar to the interface for importing images from a camera or card reader. The Import arrow shows the destination, and you can select the images individually or as an entire folder. Importing through this method also allows you to alter the image information, metadata, and Auto-Stack slider using the same methods that you employed earlier.

TIP ▶ You can also import images using the drag-and-drop method. Open a Finder window and drag the images directly to a project in the Aperture Projects panel.

2

Goals

Group similar images into stacks and auto-stacks

Create projects and albums

Use the Loupe and Zoom tools effectively

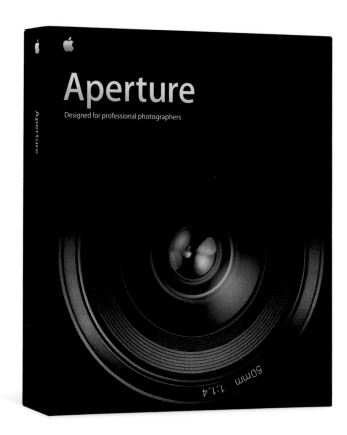

Lesson 2
Organizing Images

After any shoot, it's not uncommon for a photographer to sort through hundreds or even thousands of images for a project. Aperture gives you an efficient, intelligent way to deal with large numbers of RAW images at full resolution with incredible display speed.

For this project, we'll use a wonderful sample shoot of a Tibetan wedding party. Since you already loaded the images when you first opened Aperture, the first thing you'll want to do is identify the best images and group them in usable ways.

Let's start by creating a new album and comparing and grouping some of the sample images. Then we'll take a close look at two valuable tools for editing any photoshoot: Zoom and the Loupe.

Creating Folders, Albums, and Browser Views

Projects form the basic organizational structure in Aperture. Each project can contain a number of elements, such as albums, web gallery albums, journals, book layouts, and Light Table sessions. (We'll discuss each of these elements in the course of the three tutorials.)

The first step is to create a new album for our images. Albums are a convenient way to separate images into categories. You might use albums to identify locations, events, or jobs. For example, you could create one album for a photoshoot in Australia, another for a wedding client's approval, and a third for images that need retouching.

1   In the Projects panel, click on the Tibet project icon and then choose File > New > Album to create a new empty album within the Tibet project. (You can also click the blue New Album icon on the toolbar.)

2   Name the new album *Tibet Selections* and press Return.

3   Click the Tibet project icon again.

You are viewing your images as thumbnails in grid view. Let's change the Browser to list view. You can see a great deal of information about your images in list view.

4   Click the List View button above the Browser to display the elements of the Tibet project as a list.

5   Click the Project Management Layout button on the toolbar in the upper-right corner of the interface.

The layout view increases the area of the Browser, making it easier to view and make Browser selections. You can arrange your images by clicking any of the column headings. To rearrange headings, simply drag one heading to another column location.

6   Choose Edit > Select All, to select all the images.

7   Drag all the images to the Tibet Selections album icon, and release the mouse button. The selected images will be added to the Tibet Selections album.

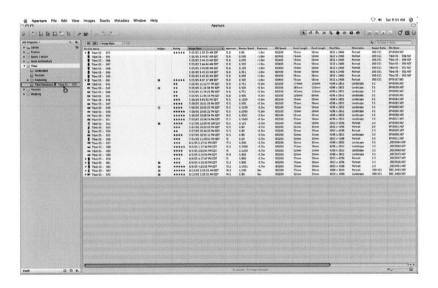

8   Click the Standard Layout button on the toolbar in the upper-right corner
    of the interface to return to the default layout.

9   Click the Grid View button above the Browser to return to the grid view.

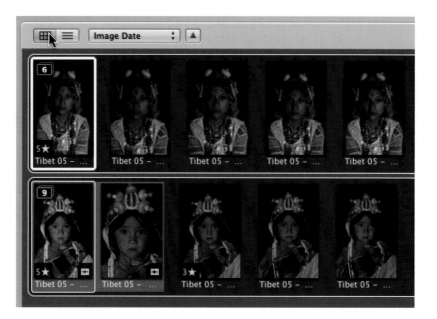

TIP ▶ You can increase and decrease the size of the Browser thumbnail
display by dragging the slider on the lower-right side of the Browser.

10 Hover over an image in the Viewer. You will notice a floating palette.
    These are called tooltips and they display image metadata. Tooltips are
    useful to toggle on and off by pressing T.

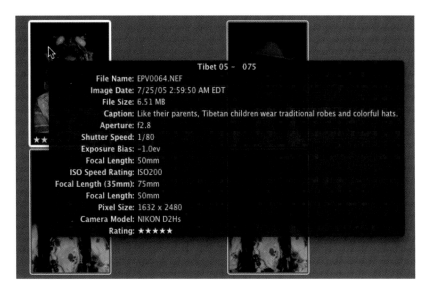

It's important to understand that an image in an album always refers to its original master file, which is safely located in the master Library. You can easily exchange images between projects or albums by dragging them from one project or album to another. You can also make new albums from selections of images. To do this, select a group of images and press Command-L.

> **TIP** ▸ You can open multiple projects by pressing Command and clicking a project icon. All open projects are displayed in the Browser under separate tabs.

Folders can be useful for grouping projects and albums together. This is called *nesting* your projects.

1   Click the Tibet project icon to select it from the Projects panel.

2   Choose File > New Folder (or press Command-Shift-N) to create a new folder inside the Tibet project.

3   Name the new folder *Tibet Albums,* then press Return.

Once you have created a folder, you can add elements by dragging them to the icon of the folder.

4   Drag your Tibet Selections album and drop it into the Tibet Albums folder.

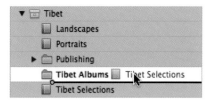

Grouping Images Into Stacks

It's standard practice for a photographer to bracket shots or shoot action in bursts. In both cases, you end up with a series of very similar photographs of the same subject, with subtle variations of exposure, lighting, framing, and composition. It's just as standard for the photographer to spend a fair amount of time sorting through that series of photographs to find the best image. Stacks are one of several intelligent features in Aperture that speed up the editing process. We'll look first at how to organize a series of portraits of a young girl.

1   In the Projects panel, select your new album, Tibet Selections, from the Tibet Albums folder.

2   From the Browser, select the image named **Tibet 05 – 095** (the girl wearing
a cowboy hat).

The image appears in the Viewer.

TIP If you can't see the image names in the Browser, you can increase
the thumbnails by dragging the Thumbnail Size slider to the right on the
lower right of the Browser.

3   Choose View > View Options.

4   Click to select the Viewer option in the upper left corner of the window, if
it is not already selected.

5   From the Set 1 pop-up menu choose File Info.

6   Choose Below from the Placement pop-up menu, then click Done.

TIP ▶ Press Y to show and hide the Viewer metadata overlays.

7   In the Browser, Shift-click on the last image of the girl with the cowboy hat, **Tibet 05 – 100**.

All the images in the portrait series are now displayed in the Viewer. You can view up to ten images at once.

TIP ▶ If you wish to make any of your layout windows larger or smaller, simply place your mouse pointer between the window and its neighbor (for example between the Viewer and the Browser), wait until your cursor turns into a double-headed arrow, and click and drag. The window will expand.

8   Choose Stacks > Stack.

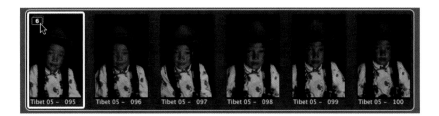

Stacks are an effective way of grouping and ranking a series of similar images. By stacking the selected images, you group them together. Notice the numeral 6 on the Stack button in the upper-left corner of the first image. This indicates that there are six images in this stack, and it also indicates that the first image is the *pick* of the stack.

Aperture identifies whichever image you place first in the stack as the best image. When the stack is closed, only the pick of the stack will be displayed. You can close and open the stack by clicking the Stack icon in the upper-left corner of the first image. The number indicates how many images are in the stack.

Open stack

Closed stack

9 With the stack open, press the Right Arrow key to view the images one at a time.

10 Click the first image in the stack.

11 Press Shift and click the third image. You are now comparing the first three images.

12 Press Command and click the second image. Now the "compare" selection has been reduced to the first and third image.

While sorting stacked images, you may want to check the detail of an image at full resolution to compare factors such as focus, exposure, and contrast. Aperture provides an extremely effective tool for doing so: the Loupe. We'll discuss the Loupe in detail later in this lesson. For now, experiment with the following.

13 In the toolbar at the topright of the main window, click the Loupe icon (the third icon from the right) to select the Loupe tool.

14 In the Viewer, move your pointer over each image with the Loupe tool and look closely to compare them. You can instantly see the details of your RAW images at 100 percent by using the Loupe. Now move your pointer over some images in the Browser to see and compare those images. You can use the Loupe on any image in any view in Aperture, even on thumbnails.

15 Press Command-+ twice to increase the magnification of the Loupe Tool. Let's promote the third image.

16 Click the Loupe icon in the toolbar to return to the Selection tool.

17 Click to select the third image of the girl in the Browser and press Command–left bracket twice. The third image is now promoted to the front and becomes the pick of the stack.

Stacking images is a convenient way to save desktop real estate and to arrange a selection of images in order of preference.

Stacking Images by Timestamp

Another great use of stacks is the auto-stack feature, which gives you a quick way to organize a project by grouping images that were taken within a specified amount of time of one another. Often this is the fastest way to group images with a similar subject matter, since images taken in the same timeframe tend to be of the same subject. It's remarkable to watch a grid of 30 images magically resolve itself into six or seven distinct shots.

1 Choose Stacks > Auto-Stack (or press Command-Option-A) to bring up the Auto-Stack slider.

2 Drag the Auto-Stack slider to the right until you reach 1 minute.

You will notice in the Browser that most of the images are now neatly organized into stacks according to when the photographer shot them.

Before

After

A few, however, were not grouped with any of the others, because their timestamp was not within a minute of any other image's timestamp.

You can always add images to an existing stack if you choose. Let's add to the stacked images named **Tibet 05 – 043** and **Tibet 05 – 042**.

3   In your Browser, drag the image **Tibet 05 – 044** to the right and release the Thumbnail when you see a green position indicator to the right of **Tibet 05 – 042**.

4   Now drag **Tibet 05 – 045** and drop it between **Tibet 05 – 042** and **Tibet 05 – 044**.

You have just manually added to an existing stack. You can just as easily drag an image out of a stack or split a stack.

5   Select **Tibet 05 – 065** from the Browser.

6   Choose Stacks > Split Stack.

The stack is split to the left of your selection.

Using the Zoom Tool

While you can evaluate some photographs by looking at your scaled images, often you will want to view images at full resolution in order to accurately compare focus, detail, lighting, and expressions. Aperture has two features that are invaluable here: Zoom to Actual Size, and the Loupe tool.

We'll start with the Zoom feature. For this exercise, we'll switch to a sample fashion shoot.

1   Press W to open the Projects panel.

2   Select the Fashion project from the Sample Projects folder.

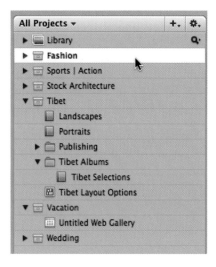

3   Press W to close the Projects panel.

4   Choose Window > Layouts > Ratings and Keywords.

Let's auto-stack the images to group them together.

5   Choose Stacks > Auto-Stack.

6   Drag the Auto-Stack slider to 1:00.

7   In the Browser scroll down until you see the seven stacked images, **Josh Session 002** through **Josh Session 008**.

8   Select the image named **Josh Session 007** from the Browser and press Return.

You have now set this image as the primary. The image should have a yellow border to indicate that it is the primary image.

9 Click the X above the Auto-Stack slider to close the window.

10 Click the Viewer Mode button and choose Compare from the Viewer Mode pop-up menu.

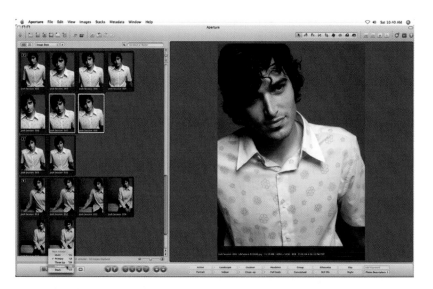

11 Select the image to the right of your primary image. Now both images are displayed in your Viewer.

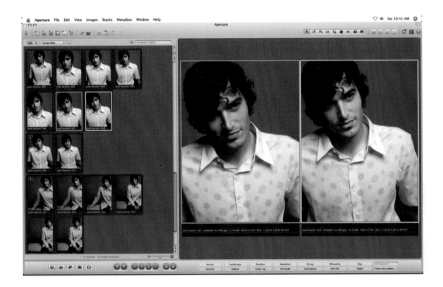

The goal here is to compare two similar shots by zooming. Here we will zoom in to check the focus around the eyes.

12 In the Viewer click the right eye of your Primary image, then press Z.

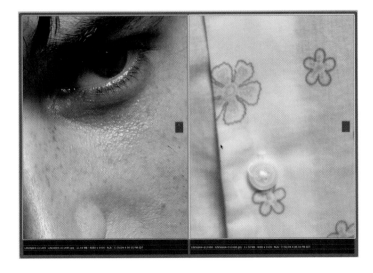

The image is zoomed in to wherever you clicked in the Viewer. Now we need to pan the zoom to a similar position on the right-hand image. You'll notice there is a small rectangle with a red dot in the middle, which shows the portion on the image that is magnified.

NOTE ▶ After a very brief pause, a proxy image will be replaced with the full-resolution image. It takes a moment, but reserve your judgment until the full-resolution image has loaded or you may incorrectly perceive the image as soft.

13 Press the Space bar, click the right image, and drag the mouse to pan around the image. Keep panning until your image is displaying the right eye of the model.

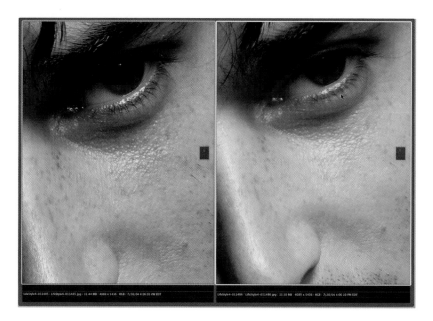

Now that you have zoomed in so closely, you will notice that the right image is a little out of focus.

Using the Loupe Tool

Zoom is great for comparisons, but the most time-honored tool for looking at detail is a loupe. Aperture's Loupe tool is remarkably effective because it's so fast and it's always available—you can drag it over any image, in any view (even thumbnails in the Browser or Projects panel), and instantly see the full-resolution RAW image in the selected area.

Let's look at the same images again using the Loupe tool.

1   Press Z to return the images to full frame.

2   Click the Loupe icon. It's the third tool from the right on the upper-right portion of the toolbar.

3   Mouse over the images in the Viewer.

You will notice that the pixels surrounding the pointer are displayed at full resolution.

4   Mouse over the images in the Browser.

Note that even in the Browser you can use the Loupe to display portions of images at full resolution. The universal availability of the Loupe is one of its strongest features. If you can see an image in Aperture—even on a webpage or a thumbnail—you can instantly check its full-resolution detail with the Loupe.

5 Press Command-+ or − to increase or decrease your Loupe.

6 Press Shift-Command-+ or − to zoom your Loupe content beyond 100%.

7 Click the Loupe icon on the toolbar to deactivate the tool.

3

Goals

Sort and compare images using the Viewer and the Light Table

Rate images using several methods

Create a Smart Album to group images by specific search criteria

Add metadata to an image and customize its display

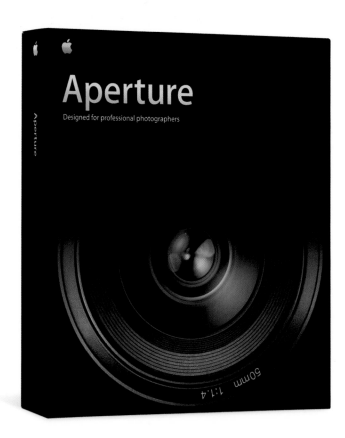

Comparing and Rating Your Images

Now that your images are organized and stacked, we can start photo editing. Aperture is designed to beautifully streamline the process of viewing, comparing, rating, grouping, and applying keywords to large numbers of full-resolution photographs, including RAW images.

In this lesson, you'll start by comparing images first in the Viewer and then in the Light Table. Next, you'll assign simple and advanced ratings to images. Finally, you'll add keywords and metadata to images and create a Smart Album to group some images by specific search criteria.

Editing the Photoshoot

The first step is to set up the optimal workspace layout.

1   From the Browser click to select the image named **Tibet 05 – 049**.

2   Click the Ratings and Keywords Layout button in the upper-right area of the toolbar.

The Browser moves to the left, setting the Viewer to the right. You'll also see the Keywords controls added to the control bar below the Viewer. This layout is designed to help you rate and apply keywords to your images easily.

Comparing Images in the Viewer

Now that our workspace is set, let's take a look at your options for comparing images. Aperture offers several Viewer modes that let you designate how the Viewer displays your images. If your system has multiple displays, you can even configure your primary and secondary displays to show single or multiple images simultaneously.

1   On the control bar below the Browser, click the Viewer Mode button and choose Multi from the pop-up menu.

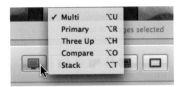

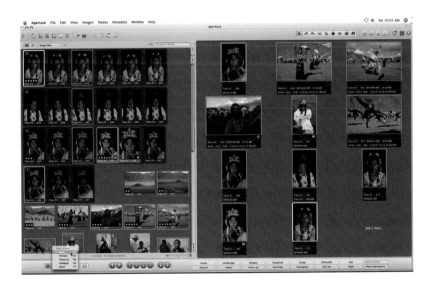

By choosing Multi you can alternate between viewing a single image or Shift-click to view multiple images in the Viewer. Select up to ten images from your Browser to be displayed in the Viewer for comparison.

2   Click the Viewer Mode button and choose Primary.

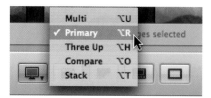

Choosing Primary allows you to see in the Viewer the single image that you select in the Browser.

3   Click the Viewer Mode button and choose Three Up.

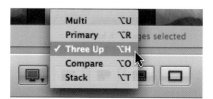

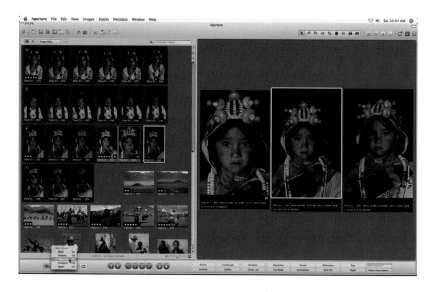

If you select one image, your Viewer will display three images: your selected primary image and the two images on either side for comparison.

4 Click the Viewer Mode button again and choose Compare.

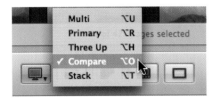

5 Click any image in the Browser and press Return.

This sets the image you selected as the compare item.

6 Click another image in the Browser.

The Compare mode provides an advanced method of evaluating one image against other images. Notice the yellow border around the compare item. Let's use the Loupe tool here to compare the image focus. To activate the Loupe, click the Loupe icon from the toolbar, or press the tilde key located above the tab key on your keyboard. Once you're finished, press the tilde key again to return to the Selection tool.

7   Press the Left or Right Arrow keys to navigate to another compare image, to see how the feature works.

8   Click the Viewer Mode button and choose Stack. Then select the first image from your Browser.

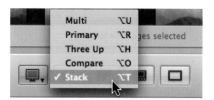

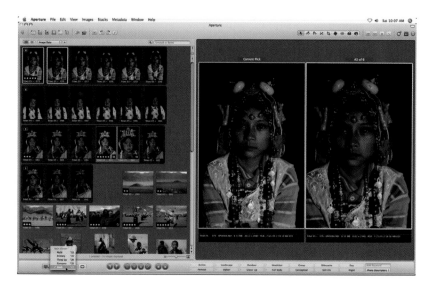

Stack is the final Viewer mode. In Stack mode, the current pick is the primary image. Although this mode is similar to Compare, it works specifically within stacks of images.

9   Press the Left or Right Arrow keys to navigate, and compare the primary pick to others in the stack.

10   Press Command-\ (backslash) to set another image as the primary pick.

NOTE ▶ Clicking an image that is not part of a stack will cause the Viewer to revert to Multi mode.

Grouping Images Using a Light Table

Aperture's Light Tables give you the flexibility to resize and arrange images in a freeform manner, much the same way you would work with slides on a traditional light table. Using the Light Table, you can drag and position your images, resize them on the fly, review your selections, check details with the Loupe, and gain a feeling for how your images might look together in print or published on the web.

1   Press W to reveal the Projects panel.

2   Click the Tibet project.

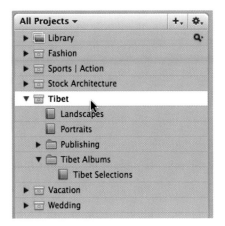

3   Click the New Light Table From Selection icon on the toolbar.

4   Click Create with All Images from the Light Table dialog.

A new Light Table is created.

5   Name your Light Table *Tibet Layout Options* and press Return.

It will be easier to work if you change your window arrangement.

NOTE ▸ You can change your Viewer background color at any time. Choose Aperture > Preferences and increase or decrease the Viewer Background level.

6   Choose Window > Layouts > Maximize Viewer.

7   Drag the first image, **Tibet 05 – 075** from your Browser to the Light Table.

NOTE ▶ If your images are stacked, the pick will be the primary image. You can unstack your images at any time. Simply select the stack and choose Stacks > Unstack.

8   Drag a corner of the image on the Light Table to increase its size.

9   Drag six images from the Browser to the Light Table.

As you drag images to the Light Table, notice that it expands. You can increase or decrease your Light Table size or scale to fit your images.

10   Click the Scale to Fit All Items icon located on the upper-right corner of the window.

11 Drag to arrange and resize your images on the Light Table.

> **NOTE ▶** To remove images from your Light Table, simply Control-click an image and choose Remove From Light Table.

Once you are satisfied with your arrangement, you can print your Light Table.

12 Select the images you wish to print by command clicking them. Click in the background of the Light Table to select all images.

13 Choose File > Print Light Table.

14 Choose your print settings and click Print.

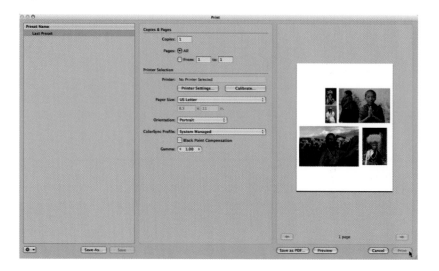

Rating Your Images

You've already selected an image as the pick of a stack. That's a great, quick way to sort through similar images. But often you want greater control when you rank images, sorting them by overall quality. That's when you can utilize the Aperture rating system.

You can give images ratings by choosing from a scale of 1 to 5 stars. For this exercise, we'll switch gears and evaluate some extreme sports shots. First let's change our Viewer to a more convenient layout designed specifically for rating your images.

1   Choose Window > Layouts > Ratings and Keywords. Press W to open the Projects panel.

2   Select the Sports | Action project and select the first image in the Browser named **VPIP3314**.

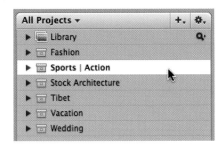

NOTE ▶ Make sure you are sorting your Browser images by Image Date, in ascending order.

3   Press W to close the Projects panel.

It'd be helpful to see the ratings in the Viewer, so let's change the view options.

4   Choose View > View Options.

5 From the Viewer Set 2 menu, choose Viewer – Expanded, then click Done.

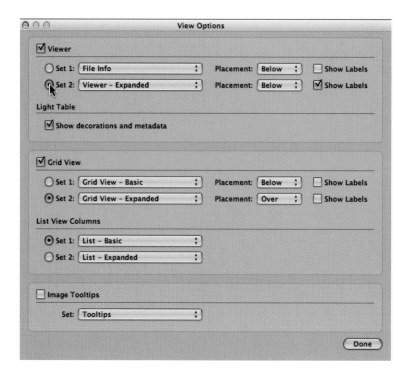

6 Rate the first image by clicking the red X on the control bar.

The red X rejects the image and places an X on the image metadata overlay.

7   Press the Right or Left Arrow key to move to the next image, named
    SC_crew_017.

8   Rate the second image by clicking the green triangle on the control bar
    twice.

Notice that 2 stars are placed on the image metadata overlay.

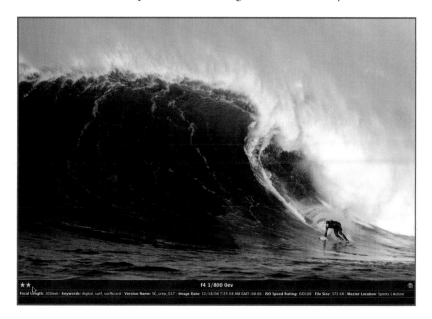

NOTE ▶ If you are unable to see the quality ranking of an image in the
Viewer you may need to enable image overlays. Press Y on your keyboard.
If you are still unable to view the ratings, you may need to enable them in
the View Overlay options. In this case press Command-J and activate Set 2
and choose Viewer - Expanded as a preset for the active Viewer set.

9 Press the Right Arrow key to advance to the third image and click the green triangle on the control bar three times to give this image a 3-star rating. (Clicking the red triangle will lower the rating.)

10 Press the Right Arrow key again to advance to the fourth image and click the red X in the control bar to reject this image.

11 Press the Right Arrow key again to display the fifth image. Click the green checkmark on the control bar. You will give this image a 5-star rating.

TIP ▶ You can also use the + and – on your keyboard to increase or decrease the rating of an image. Pressing 0 will reject an image.

Let's continue rating our images, but this time we'll use the keyboard shortcuts and rate several images at once.

12 Hold down Shift and from the Browser select the image thumbnails **SC_crew_005**, **SC_crew_049**, and **SC_crew_050**.

13 Press the + on your keyboard twice to give these images a 2-star rating.

14 Press the Right Arrow on your keyboard once to load **SC_crew_052** into the Viewer.

15 Press + on your keyboard three times to give this image a 3-star rating.

16 From the Browser select the image thumbnail of **VPIP3268**.

We will now quickly increase each image rating in a series and move to the next image with one keystroke.

17 Press Control-+. This increases an image rating and moves you to the next image.

18 Press Control- + another four times.

You can just as easily decrease a rating:

19 From the Browser, select the image thumbnail of **VPIP3268** again.

20 Press Control- −. This decreases the rating and moves you to the next image automatically.

TIP ▶ Choose Help > Quick Reference for a full list of very handy keyboard shortcuts. Learning the keyboard shortcuts will increase your speed throughout your Aperture workflow.

Using Advanced Rating Options

Now let's use some of the more advanced rating options and compare our picks. Later on, we'll create a Smart Album from our highest-rated images.

1 Select the 5-star image in the Browser, named **SC_crew_058**. Press return.

Your 5-star image is now set as the compare item.

2 Press the Right Arrow key and compare the quality of the two images.

3   Keep pressing the Right Arrow key to compare other surfing images to the compare item. When you see images that are comparable in terms of composition and quality, give those images 5 stars by pressing the \ (back-slash) key.

> **TIP** ▶ You can rate several images at once. Simply make a selection of the images you wish to rate and press the + or – on your keyboard. If a rating has already been applied, then you will simply incrementally increase or decrease the original rating.

4   Sort the images in your Browser by choosing Rating from the pop-up menu.

5   Click the downward-facing arrow next to the Rating pop-up menu to sort images in descending order.

Since you've given a group of images 5 stars, you can now take advantage of your rating system by creating a Smart Album.

Creating a Smart Album

Smart Albums are an intuitive way to organize images. Think of them as dynamic collections of images based on one or more criteria that you specify. Smart Albums are specially designed to use and sort images according to criteria entered in the Query HUD (heads-up display), a floating panel with flexible search options. You can choose a search range from one project to the entire Library of images. The contents of a Smart Album will automatically change to include images as they meet your specified criteria.

1   Press W to open the Projects panel.

2   Click the New Smart Album button in the toolbar.

3   Name the Smart Album *5 Star Surfing*, then press Return.

4   In the Query HUD that is directly to the right of the Smart Album, click the checkbox to select Rating.

5   Drag the Rating slider to the right until 5 stars are selected.

Notice that as you drag the slider the Smart Album displays only those images that have a 5-star rating. If you give more images in the Sports | Action project 5 stars, then they will dynamically be added to your 5 Star Surfing Smart Album.

6   Click the + button (in the upper right of the HUD window) to bring up the HUD pop-up window. Select Date.

You have added a date criterion to the HUD and this allows you to further sort images by a date value. You can add other search and sorting criteria at any time and your Smart Album will automatically update.

7   Click on the Date criterion to activate it.

8   Choose Capture Hour of Day from the HUD pop-up menu and enter *8* in the hours field.

9 Click the Query HUD close button (the X at the upper-left corner of the panel).

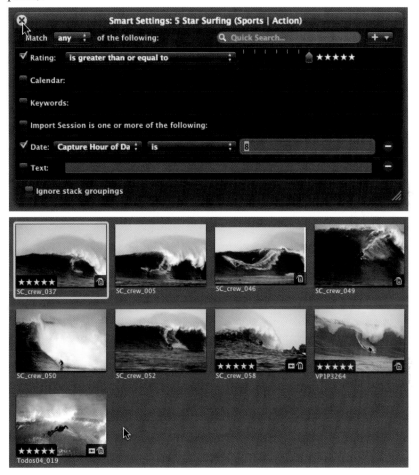

Your Smart Album content has changed to reflect the additional search criterion. It has updated and now contains images with 5 stars *and* images that were captured at a 8 a.m. You can generate highly refined search criteria using the Query HUD.

NOTE ▸ The default behavior of the Query HUD is to find images that meet "any" of its criteria. If you need to isolate images based on the criteria you set, change the Match pop-up from Any to All.

The Query HUD is not limited to Smart Albums. You can also use this highly sophisticated search utility in the Browser and the Library. The Query HUD works exactly the same way in all three areas. You can access the Query HUD by selecting where you wish to search and pressing Option-F or by simply clicking a Magnifying Glass icon.

You can gain even greater control over your Query HUD selections by adding keywords and customizing your image metadata.

Adding and Editing Keywords and Metadata

While ratings are useful for evaluating the *quality* of images, keywords are essential for evaluating the *content* of images. In Aperture, keywords are added to image versions and saved as metadata. You can use keywords to easily search your Library and even export the keywords as IPTC data.

NOTE ▸ If you are planning to export your keywords as IPTC data, make sure your keywords are no more than 64 characters in length. Longer keyword phrases may not be displayed correctly in other IPTC editors or operating systems.

Adding keywords to your images is as simple as applying ratings.

1 If it is not already selected, click to select the 5 Star Surfing Smart Album.

NOTE ▸ Make sure your Browser is sorting by Image Date, in ascending order.

2   From your Smart Album select the image named **SC_crew_058**.

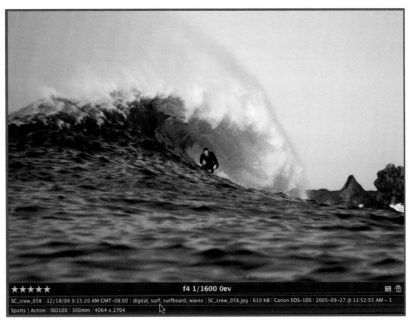

Look at the metadata overlays below the image. This image has the keywords *digital, surf, surfboard* and *waves* added. You can add keywords from the selection of keyword presets below the Viewer, and you can also add your own.

TIP ▸ The keyword buttons below the Viewer are numbered 1-8. You can easily access their corresponding keyboard shortcuts by pressing 1-8 on your main keyboard (not the numeric keypad). If you wish to change the preset keyword buttons, simply click the Preset pop-up below the Add Keyword button and choose from another preset, or select Edit to add your own.

NOTE ▶ If you cannot see your Viewer metadata overlays, press Y. If you would like to adjust which metadata are displayed, press Command-J and change the Viewer preferences in the View Options window.

3 Enter the surfer's name, *Dave*, in the Add Keyword field and press Return.

The keyword *Dave* has been added to the image. Although the control bar is a convenient means of adding keywords, for more flexibility you may prefer to use the Keywords HUD.

4 Click the image in the Viewer and then press Shift-H to reveal the Keywords HUD.

In the HUD, each preset category is listed as a separate line item. You can also use the HUD to search for keywords you'd like to apply. This helps keep consistency in your keyword naming.

The left-hand Add (+) buttons at the base of the HUD allow you to add new keywords, or even create subcategories for existing keywords. The right-hand buttons provide easy access for importing and exporting keywords.

5 Click the disclosure triangle to the left of the preset "Photo specs" category.

6 Click the disclosure triangle to the left of the preset "Image type" category.

7 Drag the word *Action* from the Keywords HUD and drop it directly on the image in the Viewer.

The keyword *Action* has been applied to the image. You can also drag keywords to thumbnails in the Browser.

TIP You can select multiple keywords in the HUD, and then apply them to one or more images by dragging them to the selected thumbnails in the Browser. To make continuous keyword selections, press the Shift key while you select; for discontinuous selections, press the Command key.

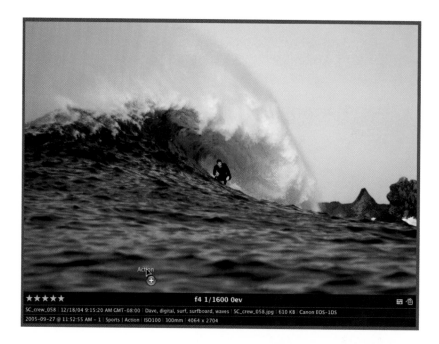

8 Click the X in the upper left of the Keywords HUD to close the HUD.

9   Press I to open the Metadata Inspector.

You can view and edit all of your image metadata through this window, including image keywords.

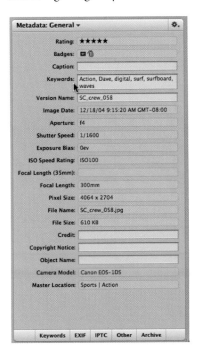

The Metadata Inspector is a flexible tool that allows a great deal of control and access to your image metadata.

4

Goals

Understand how to save, restore, and protect your image archive
from data loss

Master archive and backup techniques using the vault

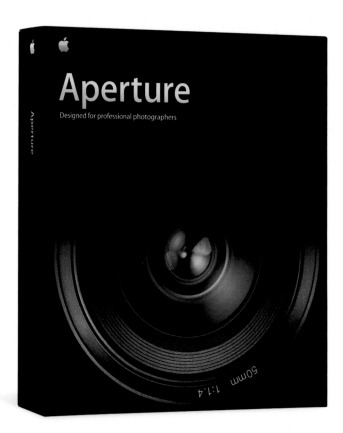

Saving and Archiving

Every photographer knows it is essential to have a safeguard against data loss—a fail-safe way to protect your valuable images from drive failure. Fortunately, Aperture has an advanced method of archiving your entire Library.

Called the *vault*, the feature works by creating a mirror image of your Library on an external device, such as a FireWire drive. You can connect multiple drives and set up as many vaults as necessary. The Vault update is cumulative, so once you have performed your first backup, Aperture will automatically back up only those files that have changed in the master Library.

Setting Up a Vault

1   Choose Window > Layouts > Standard (or press Shift-Option-S) to return
    to the Standard layout.

2   Connect your external drive.

3   Below the Projects panel click the Show/Hide Vaults button.

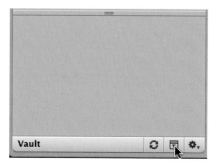

4   Click the Vault Action pop-up menu and choose Add Vault.

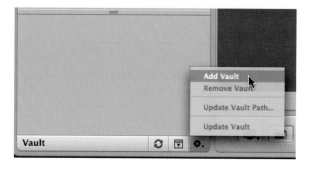

5   Enter a name for your vault and navigate to the destination drive, then
click Add.

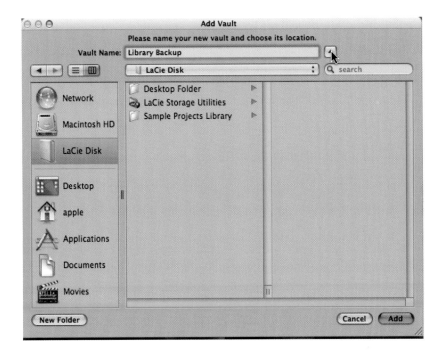

NOTE ▶   It's best to use a high-capacity, reliable external device like a
FireWire drive. You cannot set a DVD as a vault, nor can your Library
exceed your external drive capacity. Dedicate an entire drive as your vault
and remember to buy a drive with enough room for your entire Library
and enough space to allow your Library to expand.

6   Look at the Vault section. Your new vault has been added with an indica-
tion of available space.

7 Click the Update Vault button and confirm your choice in the Update Vault dialog that pops up by clicking Update Vault.

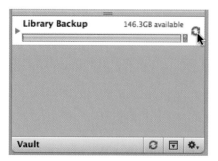

The first time you synchronize your Library the backup may take some time; however, after your first synchronization Aperture will back up only the files that have been altered.

Notice that the Update Vault button has three colors, each indicating a different state. Red indicates that you have added new images to the Library that you have not backed up to the vault. Yellow indicates that you have made changes to existing content (made changes to the metadata or image adjustments) and that those changes need to be backed up to the vault. Finally, black indicates that all changes and images have been successfully backed up.

TIP ▶ It's advisable to add more than one vault to your system. Each vault will be an identical mirror of your Library. Adding additional vaults protects against the unlikely event that your master Library and your primary vault will be damaged or destroyed. It's common practice to keep one vault at the office and another at home. To keep a second vault current, simply return it to your Aperture system and click Update Vault.

Restoring Your Library

If you change location, purchase a new computer, or experience a drive failure, you can easily restore your Aperture Library from your vault.

1   Connect your drive containing your most recent vault.

2   Open Aperture.

3   Choose File > Vault > Restore Library.

The Restore Library dialog appears.

4   From the Source Vault pop-up menu choose Select Source Vault.

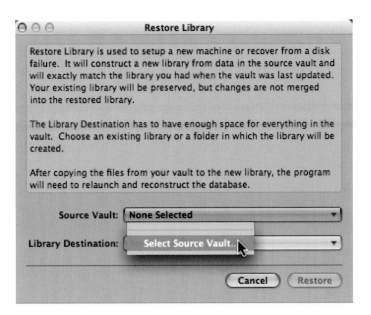

5   Navigate to your backup vault, then click Select.

6 From the Library Destination pop-up menu choose Select Destination, navigate to your desired Library location, then click Select.

   NOTE ▶ The default setting for the Library destination is your Pictures folder in your home directory. If you wish to save your Library to your Pictures folder, you can skip step 6.

7 Click Restore and then click Restore again.

   Depending on the size of your image Library, your backup vault may take several minutes to fully restore. You will, however, be able to access and view your images as they are added to your new Library.

Archiving to DVD

A traditional workflow involves archiving on a project-by-project basis. The simplest method of archiving projects is to archive to DVD.

1 In the Projects panel select your project.

2 Choose File > Export Project.

3 Put a blank DVD-R in your DVD drive, navigate to the DVD, and click Save.

5

Goals

Understand the nondestructive image management system of Aperture

Use the adjustment controls effectively

Adjust the white balance of your images

Correct the exposure of your images quickly and easily

Produce versions with and without adjustments

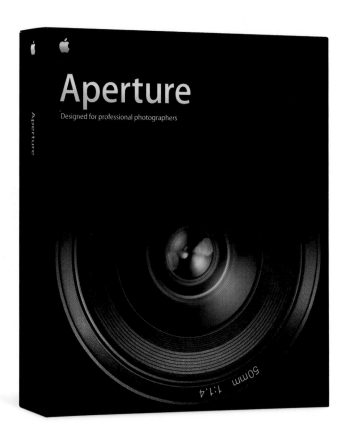

RAW Image Processing

Aperture is an advanced nondestructive image processor that supports RAW formats from all leading Canon and Nikon digital single-lens reflex cameras. You will find that you can adjust and retouch your RAW images natively without needing to convert your files, and since Aperture takes advantage of the Power Mac and Mac OS X architecture, you will be assured of fast precision control at the highest possible image fidelity.

Although it would be fantastic if you could take a perfect picture every time, in the real world virtually every image is edited to meet the needs of a project. Fortunately, Aperture ships with professional filters and effects. These enable you to make basic adjustments—those for exposure, levels, white balance, cropping, straightening, highlights and shadows, red-eye, and noise—as well as more complex adjustments, such as those for color effects. In this lesson, we'll cover the basics of image editing and retouching in Aperture. In Lesson 6, we'll move on to more advanced image editing.

While you can make precise image adjustments within Aperture, you also have the option of working on your image using an external image editing application such as Adobe Photoshop, without even having to close Aperture or move the image out of your Aperture Library. We'll address this feature at the end of Lesson 6, "Advanced Image Editing."

Making Basic Image Adjustments

Although you can access all the tools through the Adjustments Inspector, you can also gain quick access to many of them directly from the toolbar, located on the upper-right area of the main window's default layout.

From left to right, the tools are the Selection tool, Rotate Left tool, Rotate Right tool, Straighten tool, Crop tool, Spot & Patch tool, Red Eye tool, Lift tool, and Stamp tool. (The same tools are available in Full Screen mode via the Full Screen toolbar and the Adjustments HUD.)

Rotate, Straighten, and Crop

Let's start by making basic rotation and crop adjustments to a sample image.

1   Choose Window > Layouts > Adjustments and Filters to change your window to the Adjustments and Filters layout.

2   Press W to reveal the Projects panel.

3   From the Projects panel, select the Tibet project.

4   Press W to hide the Projects panel.

5 From the Browser select the image **Tibet 05 – 050** to load it into the Viewer.

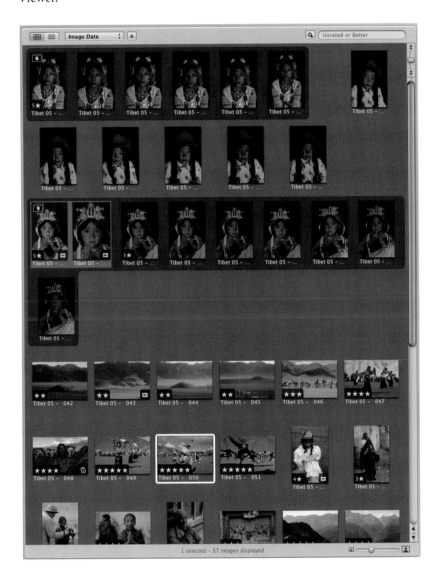

6   Press F to enter Full Screen mode.

7   Move the pointer to the top of the screen to reveal the Full Screen toolbar.

This strip of buttons is used to make basic adjustments to an image. At the far left, the Selection tool is selected by default; use it to select items in the interface. The next two buttons are the rotation tools.

8   Let's set the image above the filmstrip. Choose Avoid from the Viewer Mode pop-up located on the lower left of the filmstrip.

9 Click the Rotate Left tool button to select the tool, and then click the image.

The rotation tools rotate the image by 90 degrees clockwise or counter-clockwise, depending on which rotation tool is selected.

10 Click the image in the Viewer three more times to rotate it back to its original position.

11 Move the pointer toward the top of the screen to reveal the Full Screen toolbar again, and click to select the Straighten tool from the toolbar.

12 Click and hold the pointer on the image. Drag the pointer up and down to rotate your image by arbitrary amounts.

Notice the grid lines that appear over your image as you make your alignment. You can use the grid lines as guides to make elements within your image parallel with the grid. In this example, you can align the horizon.

13 Move the pointer toward the top of the screen to reveal the Full Screen toolbar and click to select the Crop tool.

14 Drag through your image to mark out the portion you want to keep.

You'll notice the area outside your crop selection is ghosted. You can resize your cropped selection by dragging one of the boundary borders.

15 Press Return to complete the crop.

> **TIP** You can return to the Crop tool to re-crop the image at any time, even after you have made adjustments to your cropped selection. Aperture is completely nondestructive.

Removing Red-Eye

Sure, it's basic, but there's always one shot where everything is fantastic except that your subject has flash-induced red eyes. Aperture ships with a red-eye removal tool that eliminates the problem.

Follow these steps on your own red-eye photo.

1 Click to select and load your image in the Viewer.

2 Press F to work in Full Screen mode.

3   Move the pointer to the top of the screen and select the Red Eye tool from the toolbar.

4   Adjust the radius with the Red Eye HUD to completely cover the affected area, and click the problem area.

To readjust your radius, simply click the red-eye you wish to adjust and use the Red Eye HUD.

NOTE ▶ The other tools on the toolbar are the Spot & Patch, Lift, and Stamp tools. Each of these is covered in Lesson 6.

Setting the White Balance

For this exercise, let's exit the Full Screen mode and work with the Adjustments Inspector to adjust the white balance of another image.

The white-balance filter is extremely powerful when used with RAW image data. Since Aperture is nondestructive, you can adjust the white point of RAW images at any time without degrading the original master file.

1   Press F to exit Full Screen mode.

2   If your window arrangement has been altered, choose Window > Layouts > Adjustments and Filters to change your window to the Adjustments and Filters layout.

3   Click anywhere in the Browser to make it active and press Command-A to select all the images.

4   Choose Stacks > Unstack, to unstack the images, as we will work with them individually during this exercise.

5   From the Browser, click to select **Tibet 05 – 096**.

6   To the right of the Viewer is the Adjustments Inspector. Click the disclo-
    sure triangle next to Exposure and White Balance to open the controls.

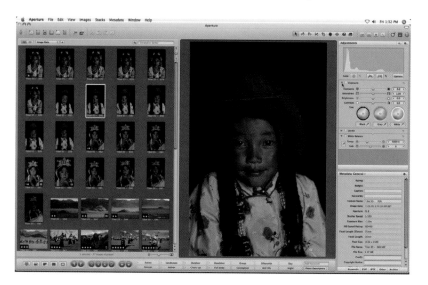

You can access the filters and effects through an Adjustments HUD
(heads-up display) or through the Adjustments Inspector.

The Adjustments Inspector shows a histogram revealing the distribution of luminance. You can also choose to view RGB color values in your image. Below the histogram are the basic filters that are always visible in the Adjustments Inspector: exposure, levels, and white balance. Notice that they are inactive by default. They become active as soon as you make adjustments to any of their controls.

NOTE ▸ A HUD (heads-up display) is a floating control panel that can be placed anywhere onscreen. It allows you to design your own workspace.

Let's make a little more room in our Adjustments pane before we begin altering the image.

7   Place your pointer between the Adjustments Inspector and the Metadata Inspector panes. Click and drag downward to expand the Adjustments Inspector pane.

8 In the Adjustments Inspector, click the eye dropper beneath the White Balance check box.

9 Mouse over your image to identify a white point. Try a white area of her eye, or her shirt.

A special picking Loupe appears with a small center square indicating the pixel samples.

10 Click to select a white point.

Look at the White Balance filter. The Temperature slider has moved. You can also manually move the slider to visually set a temperature for an image. You can return to the image at any time to adjust the white balance.

NOTE ► Although you may find the White Balance filter is useful for images that were not acquired as RAW files, you will also observe that more extreme changes may begin to noticeably affect the quality of such images.

Adjusting the Exposure

The image you have been working with is slightly underexposed. You can quickly adjust the exposure of the image with the Exposure slider.

1   In the Adjustments Inspector, drag the Exposure slider in the Exposure adjustment controls to the right. You will notice a vast improvement in the image exposure.

Before

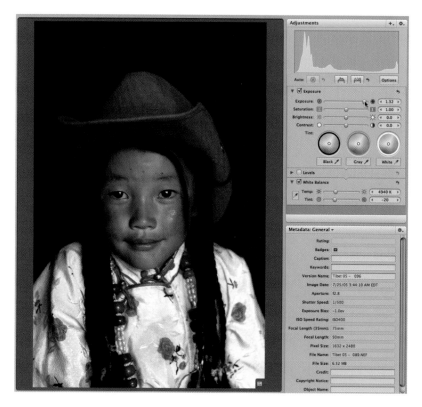

After

TIP ▶ To reset a filter back to its default, simply click the Reset button
(the curved arrow pointing left) on the right side of the filter name. If you
wish to temporarily disable one of the filters you've already applied, just
deselect it. To completely remove all adjustments from an image, choose
Action > Remove All Adjustments from the upper-right corner of the
Adjustments Inspector.

Versioning

Remember that the original RAW image has not been altered. Rather, a reference file—called a *version* of the digital master file—has been created with the adjustment information (refer to the section "Master Image vs. Versions" in Lesson 1 for a more complete explanation). It's important to understand that the original digital image is never modified in Aperture. Whenever you modify an image, the changes are stored in a version of the master file. Versions tell Aperture how to build and apply adjustments to an image. They contain all the instructions Aperture needs to transform a master file when displaying the versions onscreen, printing them, or exporting them, but they are not copies of the master file, and therefore have relatively small file sizes.

Since you can create as many versions of your images as you like without using valuable storage, you can experiment with unprecedented freedom.

You can create new versions in two ways: You can duplicate the changes and create a version that includes your previous adjustments, or you can create a version without adjustments. Let's experiment by creating some versions of our sample image.

1   Select **Tibet 05 – 096** in the Browser and choose Images > Duplicate Version.

A new version of the image is created that maintains the adjustments you have already made. This is useful if you like your adjustments so far, but you want to experiment by pushing them a little further. You will also notice that as soon as you create another version, it is labeled Version 2 and added to the stack.

You can also create a new version based upon the original master image.

2   Click to select the first image in the stack. Choose Images > New Version from Master.

A new version of the image is created without any of the adjustments. Here you can start from scratch, making adjustments and experimenting in a completely different direction.

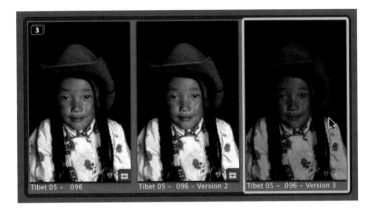

6

Goals

Retouch images and repair blemishes using the Spot & Patch tool

Understand batch processing using Lift and Stamp

Edit images in Adobe Photoshop or other external editors from within Aperture

Apply advanced color effects to images

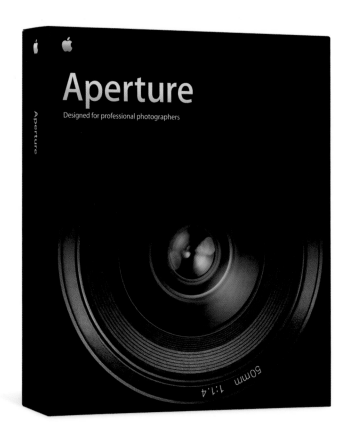

Advanced Image Editing

The basic adjustment tools we've covered so far—Rotate Left, Rotate Right, Straighten, Crop, Red Eye, White Balance, and Exposure—are just the tip of the iceberg. Aperture ships with other professional filters and effects, including those for highlights and shadows, noise reduction, color effects, and more.

We'll take a look here at the Spot & Patch tool, which gives you precision control for flawless blends, and the Lift and Stamp tools, which enable you to batch-process your adjustments. Then we'll move on to some more advanced filters and effects.

Spot & Patch

Many times you'll need to remove a spot or blemish from an image. The Spot & Patch tool was designed to automatically remove blemishes from an image either by blending the surrounding image texture (spotting) or by cloning pixels from another part of the image to repair the problem area (patching). Let's start by using the Spot tool to remove a blemish by blending nearby pixels.

1   Choose Stacks > Open Stack and select the first image in the stack, the one where you applied an exposure adjustment.

2   Press F to enter Full Screen mode.

3   Press H to open the Adjustments HUD. Place your cursor over her middle freckle and press Z.

    This zooms the image to 100%. It's much easier to make adjustments when you're closer to your image. If you press the Space bar and drag, you can manually navigate around your image.

4   Select Spot & Patch from the Add Adjustments pop-up menu on the Adjustments HUD.

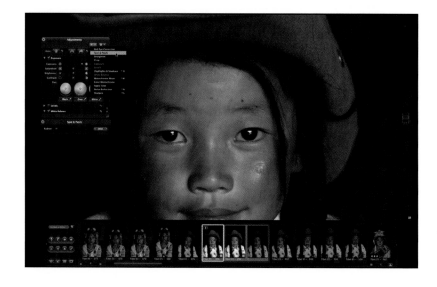

The Spot & Patch parameters are added to the Adjustments HUD. You will notice that a small Spot & Patch window also opens with a Radius control. Use this Radius control to adjust the radius of your selection area.

5 Click to select the middle freckle on the girl's forehead.

6 In the Adjustments HUD, drag the Radius slider to the left until the Radius reads 14.00. Adjust the Softness to 61%, and the Detail to 77.

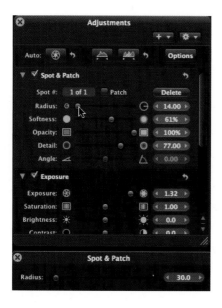

The freckle is replaced with pixel data from the surrounding area of the image to create a seamless blend.

TIP You can numerically enter adjustments, or you can increase and decrease the parameters by single increments by clicking on the left and right arrows to the right of the slider.

7 Now let's repair a blemish by patching. Drag the Spot & Patch Radius slider to a value of 17. This will set the initial radius. Click another freckle on the girl's forehead.

8 Option-click a spot of her skin next to the freckle. The goal here is to choose a clone source for your patch that closely resembles the area you wish to cover.

A second, linked white circle appears. This second circle is the clone source. You can drag the second circle to change the clone source for the patch.

9 Drag the Softness slider to the right to increase the softness of the Patch.

You can also increase the radius of the patch, and the opacity, angle, and detail of the spot and patch, using the controls in the Adjustments HUD. To access the properties of an earlier spot or patch, simply click the circle and change the parameters in the HUD. Experiment with the patch controls until you're satisfied with your retouching work on the freckle.

Now let's retouch another blemish using both the Spot and Patch tools. We'll start by examining the image using the Loupe.

10 Press Z key to exit the Zoom. Move your pointer to the top of the screen to bring up the toolbar, and click the Loupe button to select the Loupe tool.

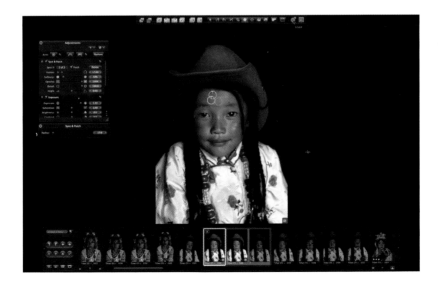

11 Mouse over her left cheek and you will notice a white mark on the image.

12 Click the Loupe tool button in the toolbar to toggle off the Loupe tool, mouse over the white scratches on her left cheek, and then press Z to zoom in to the image.

13 If you need to manually move your image into view, press the Space bar and drag until her left cheek is in full view.

14 Click in the middle of the white marks on her cheek.

15 In the Adjustments HUD, increase the Radius to a value of 19, either by entering the numerical value or by dragging the slider to the right.

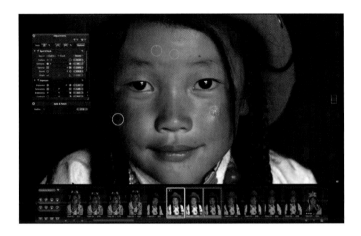

You can drag the spot to reposition it directly over the scratch.

16 In the Adjustments HUD increase the Softness to a value of 25%.

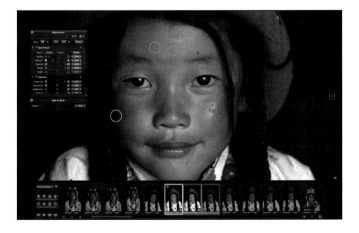

You will notice that the Spot tool isn't quite suited to this particular spot, so let's turn it into a patch.

17 Option-click just above your initial spot. Move the clone source until the scratch is seamlessly covered. Press Z to exit the Zoom.

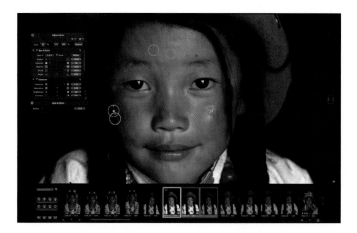

You have completed some significant retouch work on your image. Next, we'll experiment with transferring those adjustments to other images, using the Lift and Stamp tools.

Lift and Stamp

If you have a series of images shot under the same conditions, then you can take advantage of Aperture's ability to apply a set of image adjustments to another image or group of images simultaneously. You can choose to copy some or all of your changes. In Aperture, this process is called *lift and stamp*.

1   Press F to exit Full Screen mode.

2   Click the close button to close the Adjustments and Spot & Patch HUDs.

3   Click the Lift tool located on the toolbar above the Viewer (second button from right).

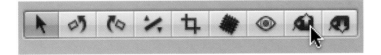

4 Click directly in the image in the Viewer.

Once you click an adjusted image you will notice that the Lift & Stamp HUD displays a list of the image properties.

5 Click the disclosure triangle next to Adjustments to view the image adjustments. Click to select Spot & Patch from Adjustments and press Delete.

You can simply select which image adjustments you wish to stamp onto another image from the list.

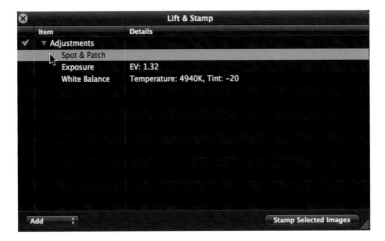

6   Click the third thumbnail from the stack in the Browser.

Notice that the cursor is now pointing down, indicating that it has toggled from the Lift to the Stamp tool.

Each time you click an image, the Stamp tool places the selected adjustments on that image. If you want to apply the Stamp to more than one image at a time, simply press the Shift key as you click-select multiple images.

7 Press A to change your cursor to the Selection tool.

NOTE ► You can use the Lift and Stamp tools to copy and paste everything from metadata to filters and effects from one image to another. Simply select which properties you wish to copy from the Lift & Stamp HUD and stamp them onto another image or group of images.

Using an External Image Editor Within Aperture

Although you can perform essential image processing in Aperture, there may be processes you want to perform in an external application such as Adobe Photoshop. Aperture allows you to seamlessly edit your images in the application of your choice without having to exit Aperture or move images out of your Aperture Library.

1 Choose Aperture > Preferences.

2 In the External Editor area, click Set.

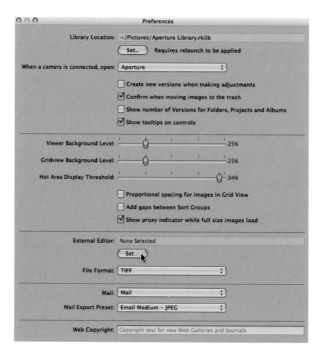

3   Navigate to your preferred application in the Applications folder and click Select.

4   Choose TIFF or PSD as your preferred export format from the File Format pop-up menu.

5   Close the Preferences dialog.

6   Select an image and choose Images > Open with External Editor.

> **NOTE** ▶ If you want to edit an image that is in a stack, you'll need to expand the stack and manually select the desired image.

Aperture will create a new version of your image, the external editor application will launch, and you can begin to make your adjustments.

7   Once you have finished editing, press Command-S to save the file.

> **NOTE** ▶ There is no need to perform a Save As operation. Aperture keeps track of the name and location of your file. The image you edit externally will be added to the Aperture Library and safely stored with all your other versions.

8   Click on the Aperture icon in the Dock to return to Aperture.

You will notice a short pause as the Library updates. Aperture will refresh and display the changes you made to the edited version.

Monochrome Mixer

Let's move on now to some more advanced color effects: monochrome, color monochrome, and sepia. We'll also take a look at the Sharpen filter at the end of this lesson.

To achieve a monochrome effect, you can of course simply desaturate your image. But the Monochrome Mixer filter in Aperture takes it a step further, offering some beautiful and powerful image adjustment options.

The strength of the Monochrome Mixer is that it allows you to adjust each color channel individually, thereby giving you control over how your image will look in black and white. Let's experiment on the sixth image in the Browser to produce three very different monochrome looks.

1   Click to select **Tibet 05 – 080** to load the image in the Viewer.

2   In the Adjustments Inspector click the Action button and choose RGB from the menu.

The histogram changes to display the red, green, and blue values of your image.

3   From the Add pop-up menu choose Monochrome Mixer.

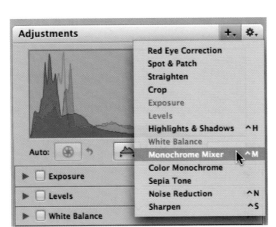

Let's increase the red and blue channels.

4   Drag the Red slider to 80% and drag the Blue slider to 80%.

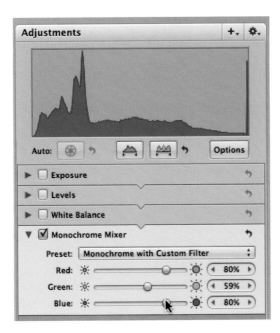

The image is now a dynamic monochrome, and it looks much better than if you had simply desaturated your image.

Desaturated image   Image with Monochrome Mixer filter

Let's compare the Monochrome Mixer presets.

5   Choose Monochrome with Red Filter from the Preset pop-up.

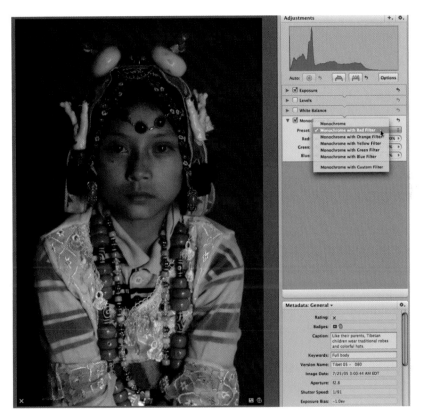

Monochrome with red filter

The preset is set to 100% red and 0% green and blue. This isolates the red channel in the image. You can also see a number of other Monochrome Filter presets.

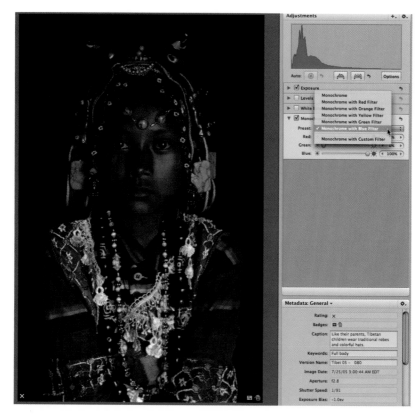

Monochrome with blue filter

You can cycle through each preset to view the RGB mix, and you can even use the presets as a starting point to further adjust your image using the Monochrome Mixer RGB sliders.

Color Monochrome

The Color Monochrome filter allows you to select any color as your image wash. You can also control the intensity of the color wash and use the Colors palette to select and save color swatches. Let's change images, increase the exposure, and apply a Color Monochrome filter.

1   Select Tibet **05 – 082** from the Browser.

2   Click the Exposure disclosure button in the Adjustments Inspector.

3   Drag the Exposure slider to the right to a value of 0.85.

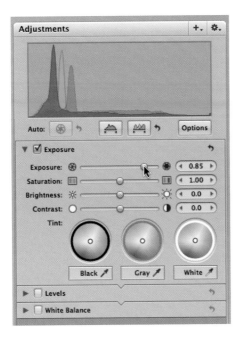

4 From the Add pop-up menu choose Color Monochrome.

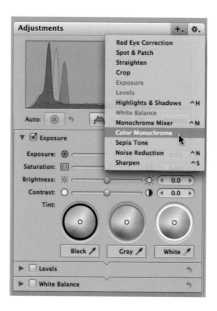

5 Click the color swatch in the Color Monochrome filter.

A color wheel appears. The icons at the top of the color wheel allow you to view your color as a wheel; as sliders representing RGB, CMYK, grayscale, or HSB; or as a palette or crayons.

You can use the magnifying glass to sample a color from anywhere on your display. You will see this color wheel throughout the Mac operating system and it's also found in other Apple applications.

6 Click the magnifying glass to select it. You will notice your cursor turns into a magnifying glass.

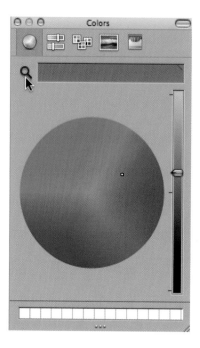

7 From the Browser click to select a yellow sample from one of the thumbnails.

The color of your image has updated. You can save the color swatch for use in the future.

8 Drag the color swatch from the color bar beside the magnifying glass to one of the white cells in the panel below the color wheel.

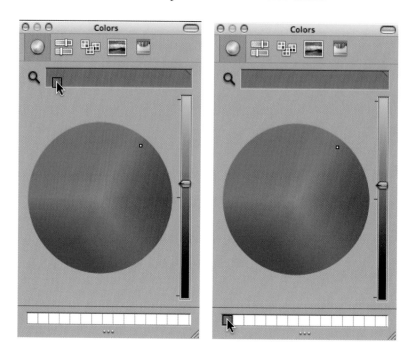

NOTE ▶ This color swatch is now available for you as a sample custom color. You can increase the number of available cells by dragging the three dots beneath the panel.

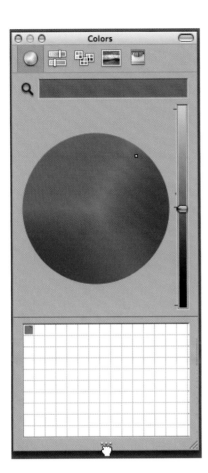

9   Drag the Intensity slider in the Color Monochrome area to the left to decrease the color influence over your picture.

10 Click the upper-left button of the Colors palette to close the window.

Now that we have applied a Color Monochrome filter, let's choose a different image and apply a sepia tone.

Sepia Tone

The Sepia Tone filter is specifically designed to allow you to adjust the intensity of a sepia wash.

1 Click to select **Tibet 05 – 081** from the Browser.

2   Click the Add pop-up in the Adjustments Inspector and choose Sepia Tone.

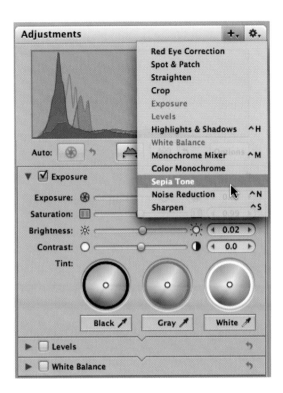

3   Adjust the sepia intensity by dragging the Intensity slider to the left until the value reads 0.8.

We have added a sepia wash, adjusting the intensity to create a more subtle color than the original. Let's take this image a little further by applying a Sharpen filter.

Sharpen

The Sharpen filter applies an adjustment that is frequently used in image retouching, and can vastly improve the appearance of your images.

1   Click the Add button in the Adjustments Inspector and choose Sharpen from the pop-up menu.

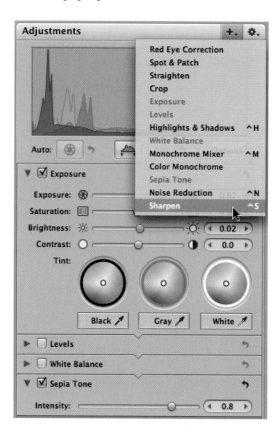

2 From the upper right of the toolbar click the Loupe tool to activate it.

3 With the Loupe, mouse over the image to look at the details, concentrating on her eyes. You will notice that the focus is slightly soft.

4 Click the Loupe tool again to deactivate it.

5 In the Adjustments Inspector drag the Intensity slider of the Sharpen filter to the right to a value of 0.66 and drag the Radius to a value of 4.08.

> **TIP** You can also click on the left or right arrows beside the numerical value to increase or decrease your value by 1 increment.

6 Mouse between her eyes and press Z to zoom in to your image.

7 Enable and disable your Sharpen filter by clicking the checkbox. This allows you to view the image before and after.

Before

After applying the Sharpen filter

Notice that the focus and the detail of the image are vastly improved.

8   Press Z to view the entire image in the Viewer.

NOTE ▶ If you have distortion or noise in an image, particularly an image that was shot in low light, you can improve the image by applying Aperture's Noise Reduction filter. Take some time to experiment with the Noise Reduction filter on your own.

7

Goals

Export images for use in other applications and for print and web output

Build a web gallery for client review or to display your portfolio

Build a web journal for online delivery

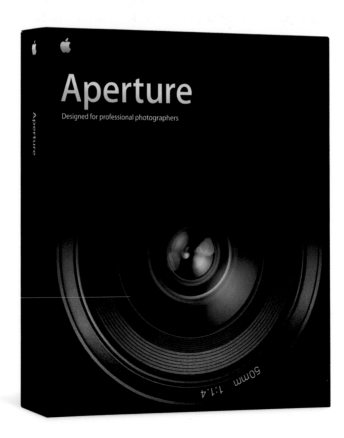

Professional Web Publishing

The next lessons focus on proofing and publishing: the culmination of the Aperture workflow. You've imported, sorted, and organized your images; you've retouched and adjusted your picks. Now you need to output your images for client review and for final delivery and display.

In Lesson 7, we'll start by taking a comprehensive look at exporting image files from Aperture for use in other applications and for print and Web output. Then we'll create a web gallery for client review and a web journal for online image display.

Exporting Images From Aperture

Depending on your project and your client, you may need to export images in a variety of ways. Aperture offers extremely flexible and customizable export options.

You can export your images for use in another application, for client approval, or for web and print publishing. You can rename files during export, resize them, include metadata, apply ColorSync profiles and watermarks, and save your favorite export settings as timesaving presets. You have a choice of all the commonly used professional image file formats, including JPEG, TIFF, PNG, and PSD.

You also have the choice to export either image versions or master images. When you export a master image, Aperture duplicates the original master file and exports it unmodified. When you export a version, Aperture applies all its image adjustments to the master image and exports a new image in whatever format you specify. As always, the master image remains intact.

Exporting an Image Using Export Presets

In this exercise, you will experiment with one of Aperture's most useful and flexible export features, export presets.

An export preset is a group of export settings, such as those for file format, resolution, bit-depth, metadata, and watermark. Presets are an efficient way to apply a set of export settings to an image or a group of images during export. Because they are easy to customize and duplicate, export presets give you tremendous control over your export settings.

Here, we'll create a customized preset to export four image versions.

1   Open Aperture. The main window will appear in the default layout.

   NOTE ▶ If this is your first time opening Aperture, you will need to load the sample images included with the application. Please refer to Lesson 1 and follow the steps to navigate through the Welcome screen and load the sample images.

2   Choose Window > Layouts > Project Management to change to the
    Project Management layout.

3   Select the Tibet project from the Projects panel.

4   In the Browser, click the first image, hold down the Command key, and
    click three more images to select them.

5   Choose File > Export Versions.

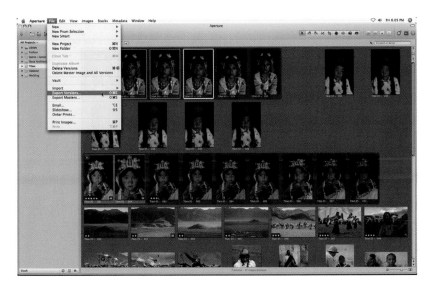

6 An Aperture Exports dialog appears. Navigate to a location where you want to export the images (in this example, the Exports folder on the desktop).

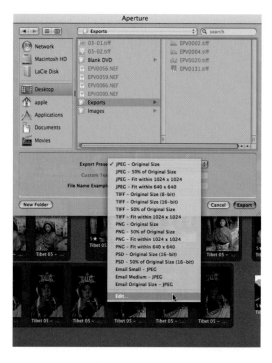

The next step is to choose the file format, resolution, and bit-depth for your image export.

Predefined Presets in Aperture

Aperture offers a number of useful predefined export presets commonly used for exporting proofs or final prints. You can choose from one of the prebuilt export presets simply by selecting a preset from the Export Preset pop-up menu.

▶   JPEG – Original Size

▶   JPEG – 50% of Original Size

▶   JPEG – Fit within 1024 x 1024

- ▶ JPEG – Fit within 640 x 640
- ▶ TIFF – Original Size (8-bit)
- ▶ TIFF – Original Size (16-bit)
- ▶ TIFF – 50% of Original Size
- ▶ TIFF – Fit within 1024 x 1024
- ▶ PNG – Original Size
- ▶ PNG – 50% of Original Size
- ▶ PNG – Fit within 1024 x 1024
- ▶ PNG – Fit within 640 x 640
- ▶ PSD – Original Size (16-bit)
- ▶ PSD – 50% of Original Size (16-bit)
- ▶ Email Small – JPEG
- ▶ Email Medium – JPEG
- ▶ Email Original Size – JPEG

In this exercise, however, we'll create our own customized preset.

The capability to create a custom preset is an extremely useful feature, because often you will choose to export images with the same settings required by the type of job, the client, the output device, or the printing press you are using. For example, if you have a client with particular image format requirements, you can edit your settings to reflect that client's requirements and label your preset with that client's name.

7   Choose Edit from the Export Preset pop-up menu to create your own export preset.

This will bring up the Export Presets dialog.

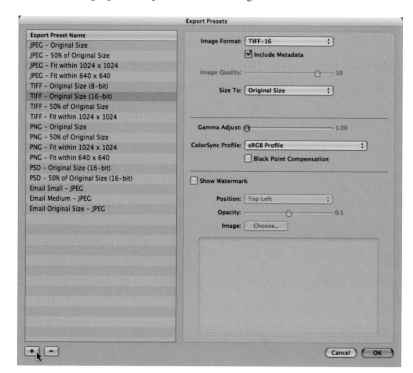

8 Select TIFF – Original Size (16-bit) from the Export Preset Name items, then click the Add (+) button in the lower-left corner.

We will base our new preset on these settings.

TIP To view the settings of any preset, simply select Edit from the Export Preset pop-up menu and select the preset. If you want to base your new preset on an existing preset, highlight the original preset and then click the Add button.

9 Name your new preset *TIFF – Client X.*

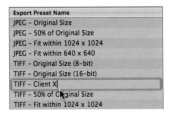

You have a number of options in the Export Presets dialog.

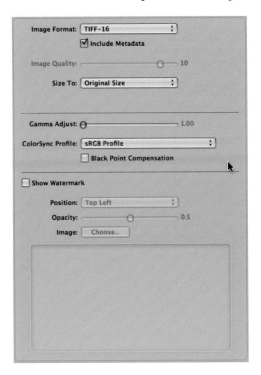

10 Choose TIFF–16 as your Image Format.

11 If it's not already selected, click to select the Include Metadata checkbox.

By selecting this checkbox you will include image metadata such as EXIF specifications, IPTC data, and keywords.

12 From the Size To pop-up menu, choose Percent of Original.

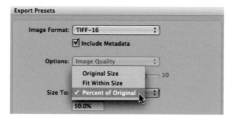

13 Enter *50.0%* in the Size To entry field.

Notice that in the next section of the Export Presets dialog, you can choose to adjust the gamma of your image. For this exercise, we'll leave the gamma point alone, assuming that we've already adjusted our images individually.

NOTE ▶ You should adjust the gamma only if you find the midrange contrast of your images consistently too high or too low for an intended use.

You can also select a ColorSync profile to attach to the export (see the "Color-Managed Workflow" section at the end of Lesson 8 for more information on ColorSync profiles). Again, we'll stay with the default here.

TIP ▶ If you do select a ColorSync profile, remember to revisit your export preset settings and adjust your ColorSync profiles when you have been given a new profile from your print vendor or have recalibrated and reprofiled your proofing printer or other device.

14 If you have a watermark image file already created, then click the Show Watermark checkbox to export your images with your embedded water-mark. Choose Top Left as the position of the watermark, adjust the Opacity to suit your preference, and use the Image pop-up menu to navi-gate to the image you want to use as a watermark, such as your logo.

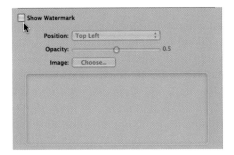

TIP Save your watermark as a PSD file with a transparent background. It works best to save versions in multiple sizes. This will save you time, as you will then be able to apply an appropriately sized watermark to your images. Once you create a watermark, you can save the appropriately sized version as a part of any export preset and reuse it.

15 Click OK when you have finished.

Your preset has been added to the available Export Preset names in the Exports Presets dialog.

16 From the Export Name Format pop-up, choose Edit.

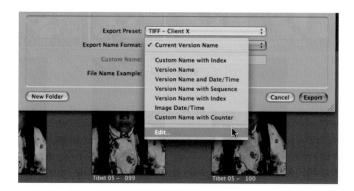

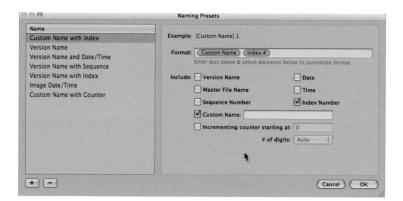

The Naming Presets dialog appears. This window offers you extreme flexibility in naming your images. You can choose any combination of available options, and you can add your own custom text and sequentially number your exported images.

17 Select Version Name from the Name presets list, click the checkbox for Date, then click OK.

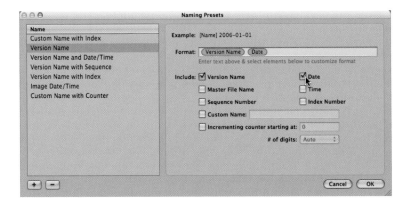

This adds a date value to the version name of your image.

18 Click Export to begin exporting your images.

NOTE ▶ To export your original, unchanged master images rather than versions, choose File > Export Masters. Aperture will duplicate the master images, in their original format, with only the metadata that was originally imported with the images.

Building Images for the Web

As online client review and online proofing become more common, it's increasingly important to be able to easily create image galleries on a website to provide previews for clients or simply to showcase your work.

Aperture makes creating and updating web galleries easy. You can create client previews as soon as you import your images, choosing from automatically formulated webpages much like an online contact sheet. You can create polished web galleries to showcase final images for a single job or an entire portfolio of work. You can also create web journals, which allow you to combine text and photos on a page with layout flexibility.

In these next exercises, you will build both an image web gallery and an image web journal. We'll start with a simple web gallery of the type you might use to post images for client preview.

Building an Image Web Gallery

1   Click to select the Wedding project from the Projects panel.

2   Click the New Web Gallery From Selection icon on the toolbar.

3   Select Create with All Images from the dialog that comes up.

4   Name your new web gallery *Wedding Previews.*

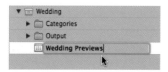

5   Click the Wedding Previews Web Gallery icon in the Projects panel to make it active.

6 Choose Window > Layouts > Maximize Viewer, to give yourself more
room to arrange your web gallery images.

When the web gallery first opens, it defaults to the last layout theme you
used. The default layout is the Stock theme. For this exercise, we'll select
the Special Occasion theme.

NOTE ▶ Aperture uses layout themes as the starting point for any web
gallery. These are well-designed webpages that work beautifully in many
situations. Most professionals will want to customize their galleries, so it's
important to note that you can refine your layout with a high degree of
control, changing the position, size, and arrangement of images as you
wish. The layout theme is your starting point. We'll explore customizing
layouts in more detail later on in this tutorial.

7 Click the Theme button in the upper-left corner of the layout window.

8 Select the Special Occasion theme from the Choose Web Theme items and click Choose.

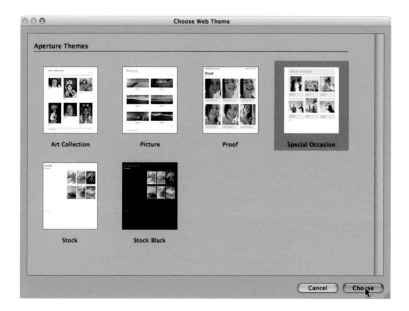

Once a theme is selected you can begin to customize your layout.

9 Click to select the entire line of text (*Your Site Heading*), and type *Sarah & Dan's Wedding* to replace the site title. Click to select the text *Your Date* and press Delete twice.

10 Enter *3* in the Columns number entry field and *3* in the Rows field to the right of the Theme button. Press Return.

11 Drag the third thumbnail, **Sarah & Dan 003** (the image of the rings), to the second position in the row, then release the mouse button when you see the green position indicator next to the first image.

Next you will choose the metadata you want displayed with your images.

12 Click the Metadata Displayed With Images pop-up menu (located between the Themes and Columns buttons in the layout window), and choose File Info.

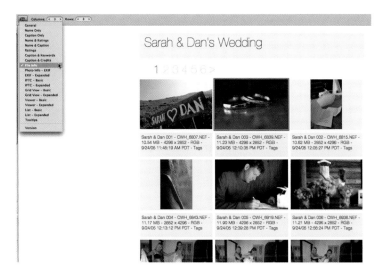

You can display as much or as little of the metadata as you wish.

Once the website is published, clicking an image will open a new window in your web browser, showing a larger preview of the selected image. This new window is known as a *details page.*

13 Mouse over the lower-right corner of an image and click the Details button (curved arrow) to see a preview of the details page. Click on Index in the upper right corner of the details page to go back to the main page.

Details page

NOTE ▶ You can add or modify your metadata at any time. Simply press I to bring up the Metadata Inspector and edit the metadata for your selected image or group of images.

14 Once you're ready, choose an export option. If you have a .Mac account, select Publish to .Mac. The advantage of this option is that web publishing is a one-step process.

If you do not have a .Mac account, click the Export Web Pages button located on the lower-right corner of the window. Your webpages are exported and ready for you to upload to your site via an FTP client.

You can also use Aperture to create a Smart Web Gallery Album. This type of album is an excellent way to create an online portfolio that is automatically updated with all your latest, best images.

Smart Web Gallery Albums work the same way Smart Albums do; their content is determined by criteria entered in a Query HUD. As soon as new images meet your specified criteria, they are automatically added to the Smart Web Gallery Album. Once you've added images that meet your criteria, simply revisit your layout and click Publish to .Mac or export the current webpages for an FTP upload. Refer to Lesson 3 to learn more about Smart Albums.

TIP ▶ To create a website portfolio that is easy to update, apply a keyword or star rating to your best images and create a Smart Web Gallery query that specifies that particular keyword or star rating in the Query HUD. Your web gallery will include only your finest images. Anytime you add a new image that meets your search criteria, it will be added to your Smart Web Gallery Album. You can update your site simply by revisiting your layout and clicking Publish to .Mac or Export Web Pages.

Building a Web Journal

Web journals are similar to web galleries, but their pages include both images and text, and they allow you more freedom to design individual pages. You can drag images and text into a page at will and then easily move and resize the images and edit the layout.

Web journals are a fantastic way to create a visual story—perhaps a travelogue—or to illustrate an article. In this exercise, we'll create a simple web journal using the same wedding images we've been working with.

1   Press W to show the Projects panel.

2   Click to select the Wedding project.

3   Click in the Browser at the bottom of the screen and press Command-A to select all the images.

4   Choose File > New From Selection > Web Journal, then click Create With All Images from the dialog that appears.

5   Name your web journal *Sarah & Dan's Wedding Day* and press Return.

6   Press W to hide the Projects panel.

7   Click the Theme button on the upper-left corner of the layout window.

8   Click Special Occasion from the Choose Web Theme menu and click Choose.

9   If it's not already set, then enter *3* in the Columns number entry field.

10 Choose Rectangle from the "Fit images within" pop-up menu on the right side of the layout window and click the right arrow to enter *210* in the width and *190* in the height fields.

11 Lasso the thumbnails of the second through the tenth images in the Browser.

12 Drag your selection to the web journal page under the text.

Your images are added to the journal. You can customize the display captions by clicking the Metadata Set Displayed With Images button above the Viewer.

NOTE ▶ You can delete an image by clicking the Minus (–) button on an image corner or delete an entire page of images by clicking the Minus button in the corner of the entire set of images. Drag an image or a selection of images to rearrange their order.

13 From your Browser, drag the first image thumbnail to the top image drop box above the text.

TIP ▶ If you want more room to view your images in your Browser, place the pointer between the Viewer and Browser. When you see the pointer turn into a double-headed arrow, click and drag upward. This will give you extra room to browse your thumbnails.

14 Reposition your image by dragging it. You can also change the image size by dragging the Image Scale slider left or right.

15 Click in the text field, highlight the first line of text, and enter *Sarah & Dan* as the title for the journal. Highlight *Your Date*, the second line of text, and press Delete twice.

16 Click the Add Text Block button located to the left of the Columns field, and scroll down to reveal the Add Text Block box.

17 Click the text field and begin typing your journal.

We began our day....

TIP You can change the typeface and style by clicking the Font icon in the upper-right corner of your text field.

18 Drag two more images to the journal to fill out the page.

NOTE ▶ If your images are stacked, only the stack picks (the first image in any stack) can be placed into the journal. If you wish to include other images from your stack, simply Option-drag the image you want to include. (Option-dragging an image to another place in the Browser copies the image.) You could also choose to unstack the images.

You can add pages by clicking the Add (+) button on the lower left of the Viewer. You can also choose from an array of actions in the Action menu (click the button with the gear), and Aperture will automatically populate your pages with images based on the action you choose.

For example, if you have added a rating to your images, then you could choose New Page For Each Rating and a new page would be automatically created according to your applied ratings.

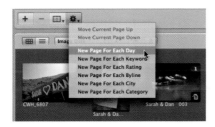

19 When you are finished, simply click Publish to .Mac or Export Web Pages, in the lower-right corner of the screen.

8

Goals

Create a customized printed book of images for proofing or final presentation

Print from Aperture using several techniques

Use a color-managed workflow through input, image management, image processing, and output

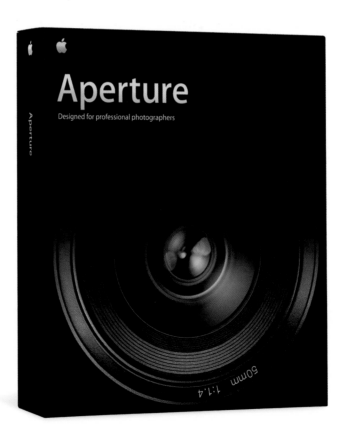

Printing and Publishing

Not only does Aperture enable you to create web galleries and journals, but it also offers professional, customizable book layouts in a variety of formats. This is a wonderful option, as you can design, lay out, and publish your own book directly from within Aperture.

You can print books for a number of purposes, from showcasing stock images or compiling a printed portfolio to producing a proof book. You have the choice of printing the book yourself or placing an online order to print the book through Apple-provided print services.

In this lesson, we'll explore some of Aperture's print output options by making a printed book and a contact sheet. Finally, we'll take a brief look at color-managed workflows within Aperture.

Creating Books for Print

In this exercise you will create a presentation book using one of the prebuilt themes as a starting point. You will learn how to add images and modify the layout to customize your book.

1 Press W to show the Projects panel.

2 Click to select the Wedding project.

3 Click in the Browser to make it active and press Command-A to select all.

4 Choose File > New From Selection > Book.

5 Choose Standard from the Book Size pop-up menu.

6 Choose Special Occasion from the Themes items.

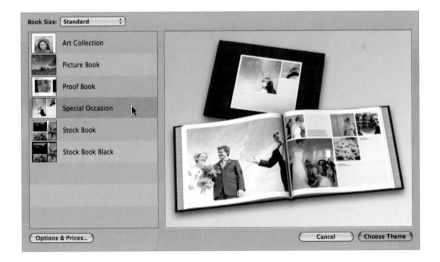

7   Click Choose Theme.

TIP ▶ Click Options and Prices for information on pricing and additional options on your selected book layout. There are many options to choose from.

8   Name your book *Sarah & Dan's Wedding Book* and press Return.

9   Press W to hide the Projects panel.

10   Choose the first image thumbnail from the Browser and drag it to the large image placeholder. Then choose the third image thumbnail and drag it to the small image placeholder.

These images will form the front cover of your book.

11   Double-click the text and enter *Our Wedding Day* as the title.

12 Click the Set Text Style button above the Viewer and choose Title Blue - Regular from the pop-up menu.

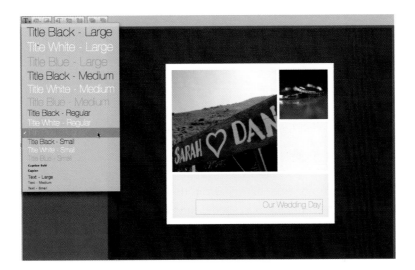

13 Click the Next Page button on the lower right of the Viewer to view the next page in the book.

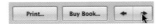

14 Click the *Title Information Here* text to select it and type *Sarah & Dan*. Drag the second image thumbnail from the Browser to the image placeholder.

15 Click the Next Page button on the lower right of the Viewer.

16 Click the Edit Layout button above the Viewer.

Your entire layout becomes editable. Notice the buttons available to the right. These buttons, in order, allow you to add text, add metadata, and add photo boxes.

The next two buttons on the toolbar let you stack photos and send them forward and backward in the book layout.

17 Click to select the *Title Information Here* text box on page 2. (You will notice a boundary box.) Press Delete. Select the large text box containing black placeholder text and press Delete.

Let's add some images here.

18 Click the Add Photo Box icon.

This action added a photo box to the book page. Let's adjust how your images will appear in the photo box and then modify the size and position of the box.

19 Choose B&W from the Photo Frame Filter pop-up menu.

20 Resize the photo frame by dragging one of the corners.

> **TIP** ▶ Hold down Shift to resize your photo frame while constraining the aspect ratio. Hold down Shift-Option to resize from the center and constrain your photo frame aspect ratio.

21 Control-click the center of your photo frame and choose Photo Box Aspect Ratio > Portrait 3:4 from the menu.

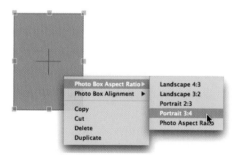

22 Drag the photo box to the left side of the page. Using the alignment guides, align the photo frame with the center of the page 3 photo frames.

23 Control-click the center of your photo box and choose Duplicate from the pop-up menu.

24 Align your duplicated photo box with the center of the previous frame.

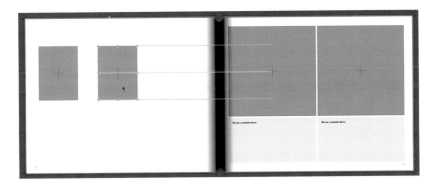

25 Duplicate the second photo box and align the duplicated photo box on the page.

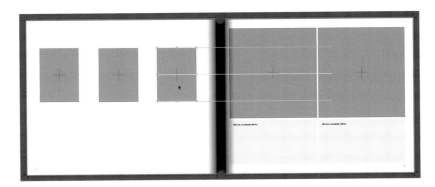

26 From the Browser, drag the fourth, fifth, and sixth image thumbnails from the Browser to the picture boxes.

27 Delete the text boxes and text backgrounds from page 3 by clicking to select each box in turn and pressing Delete.

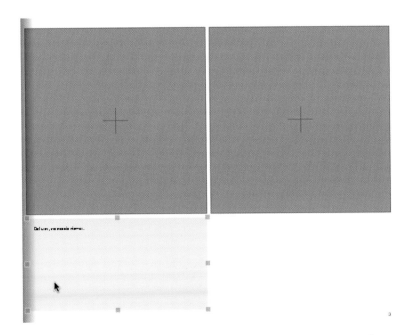

28 From the Browser, drag the images named **Sarah & Dan 016** and **Sarah & Dan 017** to the photo boxes on page 3.

To replace an existing image, simply drag a new image over a populated photo frame and release the mouse button. The frame will be updated with the new image.

TIP If you want to delete a page, simply select it from the Pages panel and press Delete; then click OK in the dialog. To add pages, press the Add (+) button beneath the Pages panel.

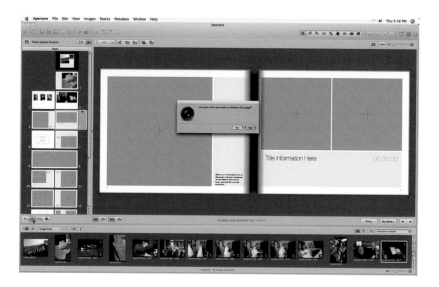

29   Click to select page 2 from the Pages panel and click the Add Text Box button above the Viewer.

30 Drag the text box down the page so that it is in line with the middle photo box. Double-click the text and enter *Preparations*.

Now that we have made some adjustments and modified our first pages, let's automate the process of photo placement.

31 Choose Action > Autoflow Unplaced Images.

All your images are inserted in the book. You will notice a small number in the upper-right corner of each thumbnail in the Browser. This number indicates how many times an image has been placed within your book, enabling you to easily identify duplications. You may also need to view your book at 100 percent so that you can check details or simply view your images at their print size. To do this, simply click the Actual Size button on the upper-right corner above the Viewer.

Now that your images are placed within the book, let's look at adjusting their position within each photo box.

32 In the Pages panel, click page 8. This page is a two-page photo spread.

You will notice that some of the images throughout your book are cropped to fit into the aspect ratio of a photo box.

33 Double-click the image on page 8 and drag the image downward in the frame.

An Image Scale HUD appears. Drag the slider to increase the scale of the image within the frame, or click directly in the image and drag it within the frame to your desired position.

TIP You can also apply an action to change the frame aspect ratio. Control-click an image and choose Photobox Aspect Ratio from the pop-up menu; then choose your new aspect ratio from the menu items.

34 Select page 6 from the Pages panel.

35 Select the fourth image, named **Sarah & Dan 004**, and drag it to the background of page 6.

36 Click to select the image you just added, then choose Wash – Light from the Set Photo Filter button above the Viewer.

This changes the opacity of the background image, creating a wash effect.

TIP If you drag an image directly to the spine of the book, you can create a unified background for a two-page spread.

A common use of image books is presenting proofs to a client. A print or PDF book of proofs is an extremely effective way to display your work to a client, especially since it is so easy for the client to look through it and gain a sense of what the images will look like when they are published. In these instances, it's useful to view metadata with your images.

37 In the Pages panel click page 2.

38 Click the Edit Layout button to ensure you are still in the Edit Layout mode.

39 Click the Add Metadata button above the Viewer.

40 Position and size the metadata box as needed.

41 Choose what metadata is displayed from the Set Metadata menu above the Viewer.

Once you have finished editing and modifying your layout, click the Edit Content button to avoid accidentally modifying your layout further.

When you're satisfied with your book, you can either print it, make a PDF, or purchase your book through Apple's print services.

Creating a Contact Sheet Preset

In addition to standard image printing, Aperture has a sophisticated, fast, and flexible contact-sheet-creation tool. In the past, creating and modifying contact sheets has often been time consuming and frustrating. Aperture allows you to create, modify, and save your contact sheet layout quickly and easily.

1 Press W to reveal the Projects panel.

2 Select the Wedding project.

3 Click in the Browser to make it active, and press Command-A to select all the images.

> **NOTE** ▶ Only the pick of a stack will print. If you need to print other images in the stack, then expand the stack, select the images you wish to print, and press Command-P to enter the Print dialog.

4 Choose File > Print Images.

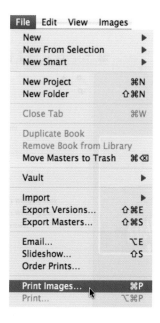

The Print dialog opens.

5   From the Action menu select New Contact Sheet Preset and enter a name
for your new contact sheet preset.

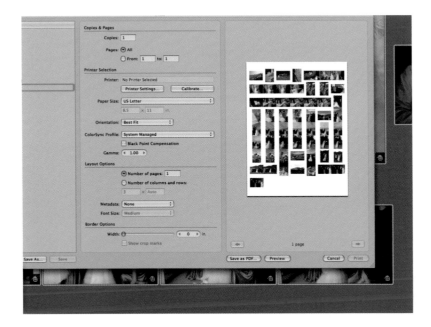

You can choose one of the default presets from the Preset pane or choose
to create your own.

6   Enter the number of copies and pages you wish to print.

7   Select your printer and paper size.

8   Click to select "Number of columns and rows" in Layout Options, then
enter *3* in the columns and *3* in the rows entry boxes.

TIP ▶ If you want to increase the size of your images, simply decrease the number of columns and rows.

9   Choose Portrait from the Orientation menu.

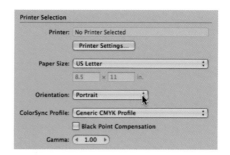

The Best Fit option from the Orientation menu will make optimal use of the specified paper size, automatically rotating images for the best fit on the page regardless of the individual image orientation. Portrait or Landscape will maintain your image orientation even if doing so creates more white space on the page.

10 Choose the ColorSync profile of your output device (printer or press), if you have the profile loaded in your system. (See the last section of this tutorial for more on color management.)

11 Select the Black Point checkbox if you wish to adjust the maximum black level of your image.

12 Adjust the gamma setting if you wish to modify the printed brightness of the image.

13 Choose Name Only from the Metadata pop-up menu to display metadata on your contact sheets.

14 If it's not already selected, choose Medium from the Font Size pop-up menu.

15 Select the "Show crop marks" checkbox to print your contact sheet with the image cut lines displayed.

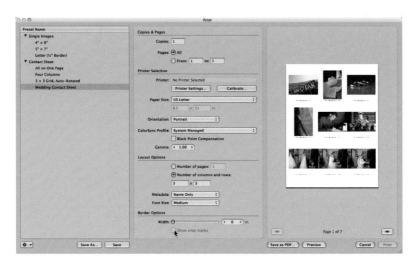

16 Click Save below the Preset pane to save the changes you have applied to your Contact Sheet preset.

Color-Managed Workflow

Color management is the science of managing color reproduction between input, display, and output devices to ensure that your onscreen display and proofs accurately represent your final published images. For detailed information on this complex topic, please refer to a book such as *Apple Pro Training Series: Color Management in Mac OS X* (Peachpit Press).

In this tutorial, we will look at some of the basic principles of color management as they relate to Aperture, and we'll learn where device profiles are stored and how to soft proof your images.

Managing Your ICC Profiles

The key to color management is accurate device profiles. A profile is a mathematical description of how that particular device—camera, scanner, display, printer, or press—represents a known color gamut, or range of colors. The industry-standard format for profiles is ICC (International Color Consortium).

Most devices today ship with a generic ICC profile, which does a good job of describing the device's approximate color gamut. The generic profile is automatically loaded into your computer when you install the device driver. For more exact color management, some professionals prefer to calibrate and profile their own devices, a complex task outside the scope of this tutorial.

> **NOTE** ▶ Before custom-profiling any device, it is essential to calibrate it. Follow the calibration instructions from the device's manufacturer.

Aperture supports both generic and custom device profiles. Like all other Mac OS X applications, Aperture takes full advantage of the Mac OS X built-in ColorSync technology, which manages device profiles at the system level.

In this exercise, we will use the ColorSync Utility to check which profiles are installed on your computer, and review how to add a new ICC profile for your display.

1 In the Finder, press Command-N to open a new window.

2 Select Applications > Utilities > ColorSync Utility and double-click the ColorSync Utility to open it.

3 Click the Devices icon on the toolbar.

The Devices window will be displayed.

Notice that ColorSync groups ICC profiles into classes: Cameras and Scanners (your input devices), Displays (for CRTs, LCDs, and projectors), and Printers and Proofers (your output devices). Your utility may also list color-space profiles for device-independent color spaces such as CIELAB.

Click any disclosure triangle next to a profile class. The utility will display a list of your currently installed device profiles in that class.

Now let's take a look at how to install new ICC profiles.

Remember, you probably loaded generic ICC profiles when you installed your device drivers. Many devices, such as newer displays, proofing printers, and cameras, update their profiles automatically each time you calibrate them.

However, you can also manually add profiles, such as those sent to you by a printer or vendor, or those you generate from third-party profiling software.

1   If a Finder window is not already open, press Command-N to open a new window.

2   From your computer's hard disk, Select Library > ColorSync > Profiles.

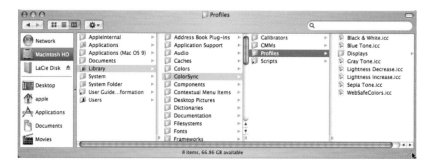

3   Place your additional ICC profiles into this folder. ICC profiles have the file extension .icc.

NOTE ▶ After you add a new profile, be sure to relaunch Aperture to make the new profile available.

Soft Proofing

Prior to printing, it's a common practice to *soft proof* one's work. A soft proof is an onscreen simulation of how your image will look when you print to a particular printer or press.

It's a good idea to soft proof your work, as no two printers render color in exactly the same way and you will get a more accurate idea of what your final print will look like once your display has been converted to simulate the gamut of the final output device.

NOTE ▶ It's important to calibrate your display regularly to ensure that it accurately represents your final print result. Invest in a good-quality spectrophotometer—a hardware calibration device—for your display.

1   Within Aperture, select View > Proofing Profile. Choose the profile of your final output printer from the menu.

2   Select View > Onscreen Proofing to activate the onscreen preview.

Your display will be updated to mimic the selected ICC profile of the output device (printer or press). Once you've finished soft proofing your images, press Shift-Option-P to turn the display preview off.

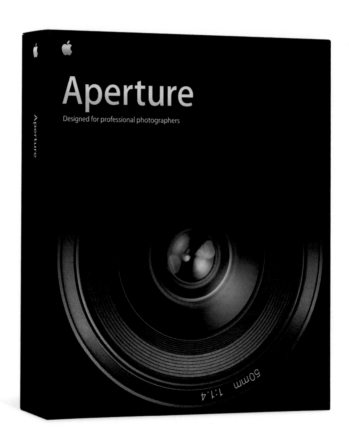

Glossary

additive color   The color space of computer displays. It uses primary elements composed of the light source itself to produce other colors. RGB is a common form of additive color. See also *RGB*.

Adjustments HUD   A heads-up display, or floating panel of contextual controls, that enables adjustments to be applied to images.

Adjustments Inspector   An area of the main window where image adjustments can be viewed or performed. The inspector shows a luminance histogram along with controls for three basic filters: exposure, levels, and white balance.

Adobe DNG   Adobe's Digital Negative archival format for raw digital camera files. Aperture supports the DNG format.

Adobe RGB (1998)   A commonly used color profile often used for printing. Many professional labs request that image files be delivered in this color space. See also *color space*.

album   A type of folder in Aperture that contains only versions. See also *Smart Album*.

alternate   The image immediately below the pick in a stack. Alternate images are used when more than one image in a stack merits the pick position. See also *pick, stack*.

ambient light   The natural light in a scene, indoor or outdoor, without additional lighting supplied by the photographer.

analog-to-digital conversion   The transformation of light energy voltage values captured by the camera's digital image sensor into binary (digital) numbers for processing and storage. See also *quantization.*

angle of view   Determined by the focal length of the lens, *angle of view* refers to the area of the scene displayed within the frame.

aperture   An adjustable iris or diaphragm in the lens through which light passes. The aperture is measured in f-stops. See also *f-stop.*

aspect ratio   The ratio of height to width of a photograph. Common aspect ratios are 3.5 x 5, 4 x 6, 5 x 7, 11 x 14, and 16 x 20 inches.

B

background   The area in the rear of the image appearing behind the subject. See also *depth of field, foreground.*

backlighting   A light source that faces toward the lens of the camera emanating from behind the subject. Backlighting makes the outline of the subject stand out from the background, often resulting in a silhouette. See also *frontlighting, sidelighting, silhouette.*

Bayer Pattern color filter array   A specific arrangement of red, green, and blue lenses attached to the surface of a CMOS sensor. There are roughly twice as many green lenses as blue and red to accommodate how the human eye perceives color. See also *complementary metal oxide semiconductor (CMOS), digital image sensor.*

bit-depth   The number of tonal values or shades of a color that a pixel is capable of displaying. The number of bits is equivalent to the number of possible tonal values for that pixel. See also *channel, color depth.*

bounce lighting   Natural and unnatural light sources (flash and tungsten) redirected toward the subject using a reflective surface to give the effect of natural light and to fill in shadows. See also *color temperature, fill-in lighting, white balance.*

bracketing   Taking three shots of the same image according to the aperture and shutter values recommended by the light meter: one shot underexposed, one shot dead-on, and one shot overexposed. The aim is to ensure the scene is captured with the correct exposure.

Browser The central storage area in Aperture, which displays thumbnails for all the photos in a given project, folder of projects, or album, including images for import. Images can be selected, moved, copied, and sorted in the Browser.

burning Exposing a portion of the image longer than the rest of the image—the opposite of dodging. Burning a portion of the image results in that area being darker than other areas.

calibration The process of creating an accurate color profile for a device. Calibrating a device ensures accurate color translation from device to device. See also *device characterization.*

C

camera A photographic device usually consisting of a lightproof box with a lens at one end and either light-sensitive film or a digital image sensor at the other. See also *digital point-and-shoot camera, digital single-lens reflex (DSLR) camera.*

capture Taking an image received by the digital image sensor and storing it on the capture card in the camera. See also *capture card, camera, digital image sensor.*

capture card The device in the camera on which the digital images are stored. See also *camera, capture.*

center-weighted metering A type of metering that measures the light in the entire viewfinder but gives extra emphasis to the center of the frame. Center-weighted metering is the most common type of metering in consumer cameras. See also *light meter.*

channel This term refers to a color channel when used with regard to digital images. Color and transparency information for digital images is divided into channels. Each channel represents one of the three primary colors that combine to represent colors in the final image. The bit-depth of each is usually 8 bits, for 256 levels of color or transparency. See also *bit-depth, color depth.*

charged-coupled device (CCD)   A type of digital image sensor that records pixel information row by row. See also *complementary metal oxide semiconductor, digital image sensor.*

close-up   An image in which the subject usually appears within three feet of the camera. Head shots are often referred to as close-ups.

CMYK   A subtractive color space used for print pieces combining varying proportions of cyan, magenta, and yellow inks to create a color that reflects the proper color of light. Black ink (K) is added to the image last to generate pure black on the page.

color depth   The possible range of colors that can be used in an image. Digital images generally provide three choices: grayscale, 8-bit, and 16-bit. See also *bit-depth, channel.*

color interpolation   The calculation of additional color values by the digital image sensor, which measures the levels of red, green, and blue.

color management system   An application that controls and interprets the reproduction of color between devices and software for accuracy. See also *ColorSync.*

color space   A model that represents part of the visible spectrum. Color from one device is mapped from the device-specific value to a device-independent value in a color space. Once in an independent space, the color can be mapped to another device-specific space. See also *device independent.*

color temperature   Describes the color quality of light. Color temperature is measured in kelvins (K). See also *kelvin (K), white balance.*

colorimeter   An instrument that measures the color value of a sample, using color filters. A colorimeter can determine if two colors are the same, but it does not take into account the light under which a sample is measured. Colorimeters are often used to calibrate displays. See also *calibration.*

colorimetry   The science of measuring color objectively and perceptively.

ColorSync   A color management system that has been part of the Mac operating system for about ten years. In Mac OS X, ColorSync is thoroughly integrated with the entire operating system.

ColorSync Utility   A centralized application for setting preferences, viewing installed profiles, assigning profiles to devices, and repairing profiles that do not conform to the current ICC specification.

Commission Internationale de l'Eclairage (CIE)   A organization established in 1931 to create standards for a series of color spaces representing the visible spectrum of light. See also *color space, device independent, LAB plot.*

"compare" image   In Aperture, the photo against which other candidates are compared when a "select" image or stack pick is being chosen.

Compare mode   An advanced method of evaluating one image against other images. Accessed through the Viewer mode, it can select any image (which it then indicates by a yellow border) against which other images can be compared.

complementary metal oxide semiconductor (CMOS)   A type of digital image sensor capable of recording the entire image provided by the pixels in parallel (essentially all at once), resulting in a higher rate of data transfer to the storage device. See also *charged-coupled device (CCD), digital image sensor.*

compositing   A process in which two or more digital images are combined into one. See also *effects.*

composition   The arrangement of elements in a scene.

compression   The process by which digital image files are reduced in size. Lossy compression refers to the reduction of file sizes through the removal of redundant or less important image data. Lossless compression reduces file sizes by mathematically consolidating redundant image data without discarding it. See also *LZW compression.*

contact sheet   A print preset in Aperture that provides a selection of thumbnail-sized images with or without associated metadata. Contact sheets in Aperture are similar in appearance to contact prints made by exposing negatives against photographic paper.

contrast   The difference between the lightest and darkest values in an image. The difference is greater in high-contrast images than in low-contrast images, which can look "flat." See also *density, flat.*

crop   Trimming part of an original image. Cropping an image usually results in a more effective composition. See also *adjustment, effects.*

D

definition   The clarity of details in an image. See also *resolution.*

densitometer   An instrument designed to measure the optical density of photographs. See also *device characterization.*

density   The ability of an image to reproduce distinct dark colors. An image with high definition in the darker colors is referred to as dense. See also *contrast, flat.*

depth of field   The area of the image that appears in focus from the foreground to background. Depth of field is determined by a combination of the opening of the aperture and the focal length of the lens. See also *aperture, background, focal length, foreground.*

desaturate   To remove color from an image. Desaturation of 100 percent results in a grayscale image. See also *saturation.*

destination profile   The working-space profile that defines the results of a color conversion from a source profile.

Detail Images panel   Area of the Webpage Editor where images can be clicked to display a detailed view.

device characterization   The process of creating a unique, custom profile for a device, such as a monitor or printer. Characterizing a device involves specialized dedicated hardware and software to determine the exact gamut of the device. See also *calibration.*

device dependent   Refers to color values that are contingent on the ability of a device to reproduce those colors. For example, some colors on a display are not capable of being produced by a printer. The colors on the display are outside the gamut of the printer and are thus device dependent. See also *gamut.*

device independent   Describes standard color spaces, like CIELAB and XYZ, in which the interpretation of a color is not dependent on a specific device. See also *color space, Commission Internationale de l'Eclairage (CIE)*.

diffused lighting   Light scattered across a subject or scene. Diffused lighting results in low contrast and detail, as seen in images captured outdoors on an overcast day. See also *contrast*.

digital   A description of data stored or transmitted as a sequence of 1s and 0s. Most commonly, refers to binary data represented by electronic or electro-magnetic signals. JPEG, PNG, RAW, TIFF, and Adobe DNG files are all digital.

digital camera   A camera that captures images in an image sensor rather than on film. The images can then be downloaded to a computer.

digital image sensor   Located at the image plane inside a camera, it is a computer chip that converts the light it senses into data by measuring the levels of red, green, and blue and assigning values to each pixel in the image. See also *charged-coupled device (CCD), complementary metal oxide semiconductor*.

digital noise   Misinterpreted pixels occurring as the result of high ISO set-tings, also known as chrominance signal-to-noise ratio. Random bright pixels, especially in solid colors, are the result of digital noise. See also *ISO speed*.

digital point-and-shoot camera   A lightweight digital camera with a built-in autofocus feature aptly named after the two steps required of the pho-tographer to capture an image. The lens, aperture, and shutter are one assem-bly, usually irremovable from the camera. See also *camera, digital single-lens reflex (DSLR) camera*.

digital single-lens reflex (DSLR) camera   An interchangeable-lens cam-era in which the image created by the lens is transmitted by a reflexing mirror through a prism to the viewfinder. The mirror reflexes, or moves up, so as not to block the digital image sensor when the shutter is open.

disclosure triangle   A small triangle that is clicked to show or hide details in the Aperture interface.

display   The computer's monitor.

distort   Performing an adjustment that changes the shape or composition of an image.

dodging   Limiting the exposure of a specific portion of an image—the opposite of burning. Dodged areas appear brighter than the rest of an image. See also *burning, effects, exposure.*

dot gain   A printing press term used to describe the enlargement of half-tone dots as they are absorbed into paper. Dot gain can affect the quality of an image's appearance by reducing the amount of white reflected off the paper.

dots per inch (dpi)   A printer resolution value referring to the maximum number of dots within a square inch. See also *resolution.*

drift   Changes in the way a device reproduces color over time. The age of inks and type of paper can cause a printer's color output to drift. See also *device characterization, gamut.*

drop shadow   An effect that creates an artificial shadow behind an image. Typically used on websites and in photo albums to create the illusion of three dimensions.

dust and scratch removal   See *Spot & Patch.*

dye sublimation   A type of printer that creates images by heating colored ribbon to a gaseous state, bonding the ink to the paper.

E

editing   Arranging and deleting images. See also *photo editing.*

effects   A general term used to describe unnatural visual elements introduced in an image. See also *compositing, filters.*

electromagnetic radiation   A type of energy ranging from gamma rays to radio waves that also includes visible light. See also *light.*

embedded profile   The source profile saved in the digital image file. See also *device characterization, profile.*

emulsion   Tiny layers of gelatin found in film consisting of light-sensitive elements. When the emulsion is exposed to light, a chemical reaction occurs resulting in an image. See also *film.*

EXIF   Short for Exchangeable Image File. The standard format for storing information about how an image was shot, such as shutter speed, aperture, white balance, exposure compensation, metering setting, ISO setting, date, and time. See also *metadata, IPTC.*

export   The process of formatting data in such a way that it can be understood by other applications. In Aperture, images can be exported in their native RAW format, JPEG, TIFF, and PNG. The EXIF and IPTC metadata associated with an image can be exported as well.

exposure   The amount of light in an image. Exposure is controlled by the aperture, which limits the intensity of light, and the shutter, which sets the duration of time that light comes into contact with the digital image sensor. Exposure affects the overall brightness of the image as well as its perceived contrast. See also *aperture, contrast, digital image sensor, shutter.*

extended desktop mode   A setting in System Preferences that allows the workspace to span multiple monitors. See also *mirroring.*

fill-in lighting   The use of an artificial light source, such as daylight lamps or flash, to soften a subject or to fill in shadows. See also *bounce lighting, color temperature, white balance.*

F

film   A flexible transparent base coated with a light-sensitive emulsion capable of recording images. See also *emulsion.*

filmstrip   In Aperture, a panel along the bottom or side of the display that is seen in Full Screen mode. It shows thumbnails of all the images being reviewed.

filters   (1) Modifiable search criteria used in Smart Albums to return a specific selection of images. (2) Effects that change the visual quality of the image or clip to which they're applied. (3) A colored piece of glass or plastic designed to be placed in front of the lens to change, emphasize, or eliminate density, reflections, or areas within the scene. See also *compositing, density, effects, Smart Album.*

finishing   Applying the final adjustments to a digital image just prior to distribution. Finishing may involve exporting a RAW image file as a JPEG for publication on a website. Finishing may also involve applying an additional gamma adjustment upon export. See also *export*.

FireWire   Apple trademark for the IEEE 1394 cabling technology used to connect external devices to computers. Well suited to moving large amounts of data quickly, it is the most common connection for vaults in Aperture.

fixed lens   See *prime lens*.

flash   A device either on a camera or attached to the camera that emits a brief intense burst of light when the shutter-release button is pressed. Flashes are synchronized with the shutter to obtain a correctly exposed image in low-light situations. See also *exposure, hot-shoe bracket*.

flat   The lack of density in an image due to a low contrast. See also *contrast, density*.

focal length   The distance from the rear nodal point of the lens to the point where the light rays passing through the lens are focused onto the image plane. Focal lengths are measured in millimeters (mm). It determines how much of the scene is included in the image and how large the objects are.

foreground   The area of the image between the subject and the camera. See also *background, depth of field*.

frontlighting   Refers to a light source that faces toward the subject emanating from the direction of the camera. See also *backlighting, sidelighting*.

f-stop   The ratio of the focal length of the lens to the diameter of the opening of the aperture. See also *aperture*.

Full Screen mode   Aperture's feature that displays images as large as the screen permits.

gamma A curve that describes how the middle tones of an image appear. Gamma is a nonlinear function sometimes confused with brightness or contrast. Changing the value of the gamma affects middle tones while leaving the whites and blacks of the image unaltered. Gamma adjustment is often used to compensate for differences between Macintosh and Windows video cards and displays.

G

gamut The range of colors an individual color device is capable of reproducing. Each device capable of reproducing color has a unique gamut determined by age, frequency of use, and other elements such as inks and paper. See also *device characterization, device dependent, ICC profile.*

gamut mapping The process of identifying colors outside a device's gamut and then calculating the nearest colors within its gamut. See also *color space.*

highlights The brightest areas of the subject or scene. See also *contrast.*

H

histogram A chart that displays the frequency with which pixels of various intensities (dark or light) appear in an image.

hot-shoe bracket An apparatus at the top of a camera designed to hold a portable flash. See also *flash.*

HUD Heads-up display: a floating panel with various options. Different HUDs can adjust levels, increase brightness, modify color temperature, assign keywords, straighten horizons, or make any other adjustments.

hue An attribute of color perception, also known as color phase. Red and blue are hues.

ICC profile Created as a result of device characterization, an ICC profile contains the data about a device's exact gamut. See also *device characterization, gamut.*

I

importing Bringing digital image files of various types into a project. Imported files can be created in another application, captured from a camera or card reader, or brought in from optical media, networked volumes, an iPhoto library, or another Aperture project. See also *project.*

Import arrow   Armlike arrow that appears along with the Import dialog and points to the Library or a project in the Projects panel.

Import Arrow button   Button with an arrow icon that appears on the Import arrow. Clicking it will initiate an import.

Import button   Button in the lower-right corner of the Import dialog. The text on the button changes depending on what is selected for import. Clicking it will initiate an import.

inspector   An area in a window that enables a user to examine and edit settings. See also *Adjustments Inspector, Metadata Inspector*.

International Color Consortium (ICC)   An agency established to create the color management standard known as the ICC profile. ICC profiles are universally accepted by hardware and software vendors. See also *ICC profile*.

IPTC   Short for International Press Telecommunications Council. IPTC metadata is used by photographers and media organizations to embed keywords in the image files themselves. Large publishers typically use image management systems to quickly identify images based on their IPTC information. See also *EXIF, metadata, tag*.

ISO speed   The relative sensitivity of film provided as a benchmark by the International Standards Organization (ISO). In digital cameras, the minimum ISO rating is defined by the sensitivity of the digital image sensor. See also *digital image sensor, digital noise*.

J

JPEG   An acronym for Joint Photographic Experts Group, JPEG is a popular image file format that creates highly compressed graphics files. Less compression results in a higher-quality image.

K

kelvin (K)   A unit of measurement used to describe color values of light sources, based on a temperature scale that begins at absolute zero. See also *color temperature*.

keyword   A word that describes the characteristics or content of the image or gives other information about it, such as the client's name. In Aperture, keywords are added to image versions and saved as metadata. See also *IPTC*.

Keywords HUD   A heads-up display from which keywords can be dragged to an image or a group of images.

LAB plot   A visual three-dimensional representation of the CIELAB color space.

L

layout   The arrangement of text, images, and other graphic elements. Aperture has four preset workspace layouts: Standard, Project Management, Ratings and Keywords, and Adjustments and Filters.

lens   A complicated series of elements—usually glass—constructed to refract and focus the reflective light from a scene at a specific point. See also *camera, digital image sensor*.

Library   See *master Library*.

Lift and Stamp   A procedure in Aperture that takes (via the Lift tool) a set of adjustments or metadata from one image and applies them (via the Stamp tool) to any number of other images.

light   Visible energy in the electromagnetic spectrum with wavelengths ranging between 400 and 720 nanometers. See also *electromagnetic radiation*.

light meter   A device capable of measuring the intensity of reflective light. Light meters are used as an aid for selecting the correct exposure settings on the camera. Most cameras have internal light meters. See also *center-weighted metering*.

Light Table   Area of the Aperture interface where freeform arrangements of images can be made. Multiple Light Tables can be saved as part of any project.

Loupe   A resizable tool in Aperture that can instantly show images at 100 percent magnification and can increase magnification to up to 800 percent. The Loupe can be placed on a single image or run across a series of images to view details.

luminance   A value describing the brightness of a digital image.

LZW compression   A lossless data-compression algorithm developed by Abraham Lempel, Jakob Ziv, and Terry Welch in 1984. LZW compression algorithms are typically used with JPEG and TIFF graphic files to reduce the file size for archiving and transmission at a ratio of 2.8:1. See also *compression, JPEG, TIFF.*

M

mask   An image used to define areas of transparency in another image. See also *compositing, effects.*

master   The source image file copied from a computer's filesystem or a camera's capture card. In Aperture, the master file is never altered. Anytime a change is made to the image, that change is applied to a version. See also *version, project.*

master Library   The place where master images are kept. The default location is in the Pictures folder of the home directory, but the Library can also be on an external hard disk. See also *vault.*

matte   An effect that uses information in one layer of a digital image to alter another layer. Matte filters can be used by themselves to mask out areas of an image, or to create alpha channel information for an image to make a transparent border around the image that can be composited against other layers. See also *compositing, effects.*

megapixel   One million pixels. For example, 1,500,000 pixels is 1.5 megapixels. See also *pixel.*

metadata   Data describing other data, including image files. Databases use metadata to track specific forms of data. Aperture automatically extracts all industry-standard EXIF and ITPC metadata when importing images and also lets metadata such as copyright, captions, and keywords to be added. See also *EXIF, IPTC.*

Metadata Inspector   Where all the information associated with an image is displayed in the Aperture interface. Industry-standard metadata can also be added in the inspector.

midtones   The values in an image between absolute white and absolute black.

mirroring   Displaying the same image on two or more monitors. See also *extended desktop mode.*

negative   Developed film with a reverse-tone image of the subject or scene. See also *emulsion, positive.*

N

noise   See *digital noise.*

nondestructive   Said of a process that does not alter an object. Aperture is a nondestructive image editing program because the original digital file imported from a camera or card reader remains untouched.

offset press   A type of professional printer used for high-volume products such as magazines and brochures. Offset print presses establish ink in lines of halftone dots to produce images on the page.

O

opacity   The level of an image's transparency.

overexposure   The result of exposing a scene too long. Overexposed scenes appear too bright. See also *exposure, underexposure.*

panning   Moving the camera along with a moving subject in order to keep the subject in the frame. Panning a fast-moving subject with a slow shutter speed usually results in the subject remaining relatively in focus while the rest of the scene is blurred or stretched in the direction of the camera movement. See also *camera.*

P

panorama   Usually refers to a scenic landscape image with a wide aspect ratio. See also aspect *ratio.*

photo editing   The process of choosing selects, as well as culling unwanted images (known as rejects), from a group of images. See also *ratings, reject, select.*

pick   The image, usually the best, that represents a stack. See also *alternate, stack.*

pixel   Picture element. The smallest discernible component of a digital image, as well as the smallest element on the display that can be assigned a color. See also *megapixel.*

PNG   An acronym for Portable Network Graphics, PNG is a bitmapped graphic file that has been approved by the World Wide Web Consortium to replace patented GIF files. PNG files are royalty free.

polarizing filter   A filter placed on the front of the lens capable of selectively transmitting light traveling on one plane while absorbing light traveling on other planes. Polarizing filters are capable of reducing unwanted reflections on windows and shiny surfaces. They are also used to darken the sky. See also *filters.*

positive   Refers to developed film where the tonal relationship of the subject or scene is the same on film as viewed by the eye; also known as a slide. See also *emulsion, negative.*

presets   Settings that can be customized, duplicated, and saved for various operations such as export or printing. Export presets, for example, can specify the file format, resolution, bit-depth, metadata, and watermark to be applied to an image or a group of images during export.

prime lens   A lens with a fixed focal length that cannot be changed.

profile   A compilation of data on a specific device's color information, including its gamut, color space, and modes of operation. A profile represents a device's color-reproduction capabilities—and is essential to making the color management system work. See also *device characterization, gamut.*

project   In Aperture, the top-level file that holds all the master files, versions, and metadata associated with a shoot. A project can include up to 10,000 master files with as many versions as needed, plus elements such as albums, web gallery albums, journals, book layouts, and Light Table sessions. Projects can also reference versions from other projects. These referenced versions maintain links to the master files in their original projects. See also *album, master.*

Projects panel   The Projects panel is where images in Aperture are organized into projects, albums, and Smart Albums.

PSD   The file extension for Photoshop Document. PSD files are proprietary graphic files for Adobe Systems.

Publish to .Mac button   A one-click way to publish a website that has been designed and laid out in Aperture.

quantization   The process of converting a value derived from an analog source into a digital value.

Q

Query HUD   A free-form search field. From the Query heads-up display live filtering can be done of any album, project, folder, the Browser, or the entire Library. Pinpoint searches can be based on several criteria, then saved for later use.

QuickTime   A cross-platform multimedia technology developed by Apple Computer. Widely used for editing, compositing, CD-ROM, Web video, and more.

RA-4   A type of professional printer capable of printing digital files on traditional photographic paper. RA-4 printers use a series of colored lights to expose the paper, which blends the colors together to produce continuous-tone prints.

R

RAID   Acronym for redundant array of independent disks. A RAID array can provide a photographer with large image libraries with many gigabytes of high-performance data storage.

RAM   Abbreviation for random-access memory. A computer's memory capacity, measured in megabytes (MB), determines the amount of data the computer can process and temporarily store at any moment.

rangefinder   Refers to an apparatus found on many cameras used to help focus the image. See also *camera, viewfinder*.

raster image processor (RIP)   A specialized printer driver that replaces the driver that comes with a printer. It takes input from applications and converts, or rasterizes, the information into data that the printer understands so that it can put dots on a page. Software RIPs typically offer features not found in standard printer drivers.

ratings   Part of the standard set of metadata in Aperture, which can apply 1 to 5 stars to an image. The image identified as the best shot in the sequence, the "pick," tops a stack. It's the only image visible until the stack is opened again.

RAW   The original bit-for-bit uncompressed digital image file captured by a camera. Aperture works with RAW images through every step of the digital workflow and supports the RAW formats from all leading digital camera manufacturers.

red-eye   The phenomenon of glowing red eyes in photographs. In Aperture, the Red Eye tool eliminates the effect.

reject   In Aperture, a negative rating applied to an image as part of the photo editing process. See also *photo editing, ratings, select.*

relative colorimetric   A rendering intent suitable for photographic images. It compares the highlight of the source color space to that of the destination color space and shifts out-of-gamut colors to the closest reproducible color in the destination color space.

rendering intent   The method by which colors that are out of gamut for a selected output device are mapped to that device's reproducible gamut.

resolution   The amount of information a digital image is capable of conveying. Resolution is determined by a combination of file size (number of pixels), bit-depth (pixel depth), and dpi (dots per inch).

RGB   Abbreviation for red, green, and blue. A color space commonly used on computers in which each color is described by the strength of its red, green, and blue components. The RGB color space has a very large gamut, meaning it can reproduce a very wide range of colors. This range is typically larger than can be reproduced by printers. See also *additive color.*

S

saturation   The intensity of color in an image. Saturated colors are perceived to have a "purer" look resulting from the absence of the color gray. See also *desaturate.*

scale   An adjustment that changes the size but not the aspect ratio of an image.

select   A superior image selected for display or for review by a client.

selective focus   The process of isolating a subject by using an f-stop that produces a shallow depth of field. See also *depth of field.*

shortcut menu   A menu accessed by pressing the mouse button and the Control key, or by pressing the right mouse button.

shutter   A complicated mechanism, usually consisting of a blade or curtain, that precisely controls the duration of time that light passing through the lens remains in contact with the digital image sensor.

shutter priority   A setting on certain cameras that automatically sets the aperture for a correct exposure based on the shutter speed set by the photographer. See also *exposure.*

shutter speed   The amount of time the shutter is open or the digital image sensor is activated or charged. Shutter speeds are displayed as fractions of a second, such as 1/8 or 1/250.

sidelighting   Refers to light hitting the subject from the side, perpendicular to the angle of the camera. See also *backlighting, frontlighting.*

silhouette   An image where the subject is a solid dark shape against a bright background. Extreme backlighting, such as a sunset, can create a silhouette effect when a subject is placed in the foreground. See also *backlighting, foreground.*

single image print   Based on a print preset in Aperture, refers to a single image printed on a single sheet of paper.

slide See *positive.*

slideshow An animated presentation of a series of images. In Aperture, slideshows can be combined with music to present a series of images for display across up to two monitors.

Smart Album In Aperture, a dynamic collection of images based on defined criteria entered in the Query HUD.

Smart Web Gallery Album An automatically updated online portfolio. Like Smart Albums, Smart Web Gallery Albums consist of images selected according to criteria entered in a Query HUD.

soft lighting See *diffused lighting.*

soft proof The onscreen simulation by a display of the output from printer or press.

source profile The profile of a file before it undergoes color conversion.

spectrophotometer An instrument that measures the wavelength of color across an entire spectrum of colors. It can be used to profile both displays and printers.

Spot & Patch A tool in Aperture that automatically removes blemishes from an image either by blending the surrounding image texture or by cloning pixels from another part of an image to repair a problem area.

sRGB A common working space designed to represent the average PC monitor. Because of its small gamut, it is suitable for Web graphics but not for print production.

stack A group of similar versions that Aperture sequentially numbers and connects to a master file. Stacks can be manually assembled or automatically created from photos shot within a specified interval (one second to one minute). See also *alternate, pick.*

Stack button Button that is clicked to open and close a stack.

T

subtractive color   Images with color elements derived from the light reflected off the surface of an object. CMYK is a common form of subtractive color. See also *CMYK*.

SWOP   An acronym for Specifications for Web Offset Publications, a standard printing-press profile. *Web* here refers to a web press, not the Internet.

tabs   In Aperture, tabs delineate projects in the Browser and functions within the inspectors.

tagged   Refers to an image that has been saved in a working-space profile.

target   A reference file used to profile a device such as a scanner or digital camera. It often contains patches whose color values have been measured. The output from a device is then compared with the target. See also *device characterization*.

template   One of Aperture's professionally designed formats. Book templates can be used for proof books, stock books, art collections, special occasion albums, and picture books. Web templates can be used to create photo galleries and journals.

theme   A customizable webpage layout that works as the starting point for a web gallery. The default layout is the Stock theme. Others include the Proof, Special Occasion, and Art Collection themes.

Thumbnail Size slider   Slider below the Browser and in the Full Screen mode filmstrip.

TIFF   An acronym for Tagged Image File Format, TIFF is a widely used bitmapped graphics file format, developed by Aldus and Microsoft, that handles monochrome, grayscale, 8- and 24-bit color.

toolbar   A strip of buttons on the default layout of Aperture's main window. Clicking them will make basic adjustments to an image. From left to right the buttons are the Selection tool, Rotate Left tool, Rotate Right tool, Straighten tool, Crop tool, Spot & Patch tool, Red Eye tool, Lift tool, and Stamp tool.

transition A visual effect applied between the display of images in a slideshow. Aperture offers settings for the duration of the cross-dissolve between images.

tungsten light Refers to a type of light with low color temperature. Tungsten light sources usually include household lamps but should not be confused with fluorescent. See also *color temperature, white balance.*

U

underexposure The result of not exposing a scene long enough. Underexposed scenes appear dark. See also *exposure, overexposure.*

untagged Refers to a document or an image that lacks an embedded profile.

V

vault Aperture's method of archiving an entire Library: it creates a mirror image of the Library on an external device, such as a FireWire drive. Any number of vaults can be connected to a computer. Aperture indicates by color which files need backing up.

version The file containing all the metadata and adjustment information applied to an image. In Aperture, only versions are changed. The master image files are never touched.

Viewer A panel in Aperture that displays up to ten currently selected images in the Browser. Adjustments can be made on images in the Viewer.

viewfinder The part of the camera designed to preview the area of the scene that will be captured by the digital image sensor. See also *camera, digital image sensor.*

vignetting (1) Darkening, also known as fall-off, at the corners of the image as a result of too many filters attached to the lens, a large lens hood, or poor lens design. (2) A filter in Aperture designed to correct unwanted vignetting in the image. See also *filters.*

W

watermark A visible graphic or text overlay applied to an image indicating the image is protected by a copyright. Watermarks are used to discourage the use of images without explicit permission.

web gallery   Images arranged in the Webpage Editor or on the web. A web gallery album is an album created in Aperture with the images for the web gallery.

web journal   Images and text arranged in the Webpage Editor or on the web. A web journal album is the album created in Aperture with the images for the web journal.

Webpage Editor   An interface that appears in place of the Viewer when a web gallery album or a web journal album is created or selected.

white balance   An adjustment that changes the color temperature of a digital image. The goal is to reproduce white as true white. For example, if the white in an image is too yellow due to incandescent lighting, white balancing adds enough blue to make the white appear neutral. See also *color temperature, kelvin (K)*.

white point   The color temperature of a display, measured in kelvins. The higher the white point, the bluer the white; the lower the white point, the redder. The native white point for a Mac is D50 (5000 kelvins); for Windows, it is D65 (6500 kelvins). See also color *temperature, kelvin (K)*.

wide-angle lens   A lens with a short focal length that takes in a wide view. The focal length of a wide-angle lens is smaller than the image frame. See also *lens*.

working space   The color space in which a file is edited. It can be different from the original color space of the file, which is called the document color space. Working spaces are based either on color-space profiles such as Apple RGB or on device profiles.

workspace   The arrangement of the Browser, Viewer, Adjustments Inspector, Metadata Inspector, Projects panel, and other interface elements. There are multiple workspaces in Aperture.

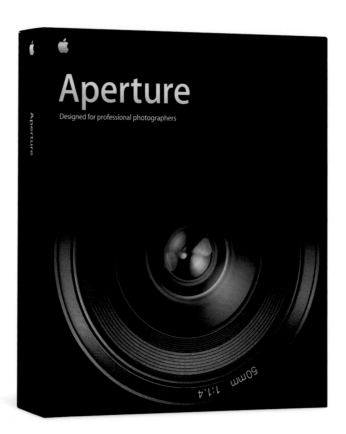

Index

The Apple Pro Training Series

The official curriculum of the Apple Pro Training and Certification Program, the Apple Pro Training books are a comprehensive, self-paced courses written by acknowledged experts in the field.

- Focused lessons take you step-by-step through the process of creating real-world digital video or audio projects.
- All media and project files are included on the companion DVD.
- Ample illustrations help you master techniques fast.
- Lesson goals and time estimates help you plan your time.
- Chapter review questions summarize what you've learned.

Apple Pro Training Series: Final Cut Pro 5
0-321-33481-7

In this best-selling guide, Diana Weynand starts with basic video editing techniques and takes you all the way through Final Cut Pro's powerful advanced features. Using world-class documentary footage, you'll learn to mark and edit clips, color correct sequences, create transitions, apply filters and effects, add titles, work with audio, and more.

Apple Pro Training Series: Advanced Editing Techniques in Final Cut Pro 5
0-321-33549-X

Director and editor Michael Wohl shares must-know professional techniques for cutting dialogue scenes, action scenes, fight and chase scenes, documentaries, comedy, music videos, multi-camera projects, and more. Also covers Soundtrack Pro, audio finishing, managing clips and media, and working with film.

Apple Pro Training Series: Advanced Color Correction and Effects in Final Cut Pro 5
0-321-33548-1

This Apple-authorized guide delivers hard-to-find training in real-world color correction and effects techniques, including motion effects, keying and compositing, titling, scene-to-scene color matching, and correcting for broadcast specifications.

Apple Pro Training Series: Optimizing Your Final Cut Pro System
0-321-26871-7

Written and field-tested by industry pros Sean Cullen, Matthew Geller, Charles Roberts, and Adam Wilt, this is the ultimate guide for installing, configuring, optimizing, and trouble-shooting Final Cut Pro in real-world post-production environments.

Apple Pro Training Series: Final Cut Pro for Avid Editors
0-321-24577-6

Master trainer Diana Weynand takes you through a comprehensive "translation course" designed for professional video and film editors who already know their way around Avid nonlinear systems.

The Apple Training Series:

Apple Training Series: iLife '05
0-321-33020-X
Apple Training Series: GarageBand 2
0-321-33019-6
Apple Training Series: Mac OS X Support Essentials
0-321-33547-3

Apple Training Series: Desktop and Portable Systems, Second Edition
0-321-33546-5
Apple Training Series: Mac OS X Server Essentials
0-321-35758-2

Apple Training Series: Security Best Practices for Mac OS X v 10.4
0-321-36988-2
Apple Training Series: Mac OS X System Administration Reference
0-321-36984-X

To order books or find out about the Apple Pro Training Series, visit: **www.peachpit.com/appleprotraining**

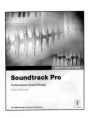

Apple Pro Training Series: Soundtrack Pro
0-321-35757-4

Apple Pro Training Series: Shake 4
0-321-25609-3

Apple Pro Training Series: Shake 4 Quick Reference Guide
0-321-38246-3

Apple Pro Training Series: Getting Started with Motion
0-321-30533-7

Apple Pro Training Series: Motion
0-321-27826-7

Encyclopedia of Visual Effects
0-321-30334-2

Apple Pro Training Series: Logic Pro 7 and Logic Express 7
0-321-25614-X

Apple Pro Training Series: Advanced Logic Pro 7
0-321-25607-7

Apple Pro Training Series: DVD Studio Pro 4
0-321-33482-5

Apple Pro Training Series: Getting Started with Aperture
0-321-42275-9

Apple Pro Training Series: Aperture
0-321-42276-7

Apple Pro Training Series: Color Management with Mac OS X
0-321-24576-8

Apple Pro Training Series: Final Cut Express 2
0-321-25615-8

Apple Pro Training Series: Xsan Quick Reference Guide
0-321-36900-9

To order books or find out about the Apple Pro Training Series, visit:
www.peachpit.com/appleprotraining